WORK SMARTER

Lowell Sanborn

BM (주)도서출판 성안당

Foreword from the Author

This book takes a task-based approach to help students cultivate long-lasting resources and skills for their futures. The task-based approach along with an emphasis on writing and self-reflection will assist students looking to venture into careers that require English Language Ability. This book has been modernized to allow students to use various devices with search suggestions. Students collaborate on achieving learning outcomes giving valuable time to practice speaking, negotiate meaning, work creatively to find solutions, and get comfortable taking risks.

Teachers and students should benefit from the short, simple instructions. Topics, rather than defined and possibly quickly becoming dated, are generated by the class itself. Feel free to get right into classwork and generate interesting discussions, while practicing vital skills for successful careers and lives.

Lowell Sanborn

Scope and Sequence

Part 1 · The Hiring Process

Unit	Assignment	Primary Goal	Secondary Goal
UNIT 1 Find a Job • page 8	Find an actual job advertisement online or select an example.	Evaluate job preferences and select a real job opening.	Analyze job advertisements and turn past experiences into valuable skills.
UNIT 2 Write a Résumé • page 17	Write a professional résumé.	Write a professional résumé.	Highlight valuable skills and accomplishments.
UNIT 3 Write a Cover Letter • page 26	Write a formal cover letter.	Write a formal cover letter.	Use polite, formal language.
UNIT 4 Prepare for a Job Interview • page 35	Practice answering common interview questions.	Practice detailing experiences without a script.	Use good communication strategies.

Part 2 · Career Success

PART 1 The Hiring Process

Simulating the Application Process

In part one of this textbook, you will simulate the hiring process. Your goal is to practice using English in the valuable context of finding work. Using English as a tool for communicating professionally is not the same as having comfortable conversations with new friends or taking a test. In the hiring process, there are specific rules to consider in order to make yourself seem like the best person for the job.

Using my Experience to "Level Up"

Career Skills are some of the most important things you will cultivate at university. The work you do here will prepare you for success in the future. Even the smallest of experiences could contribute to your career. One of the most important things you can do is reflect on your experiences and interpret what you have learned into what you can perform. This section will help you reflect on your experiences and skills, as well as teach the basics of making yourself seem indispensable to your future prospective employer.

UNIT 1 Find a Job

This unit is the starting point for your future career. Here, we will use real-life experience to consider what positions you could apply to. You will match what you have already done to a job you actually want. The main assignment is to find an actual job advertisement online or select an example from the classified ads at the end of the unit to practice the job application process.

UNIT 1 Goals

- Evaluate your preferences for a new job.
- Analyze job advertisements to identify necessary qualifications and skills.
- Select a real job opening to help prepare your résumé and practice for your interview.
- Turn your past experiences into skills that will make you seem valuable and get a job.

1.1 Discussion Questions

Discuss these questions with a partner. Write short keywords to help you remember your answers. Consider each question one at a time, answering each with your partner as you take notes.

1 What is your dream job? Why? ______________________.

2 What job do you need to get first? ______________________.

3 What skills do you have? ______________________.

4 Where do people look for jobs? ______________________.

5 What is important when choosing a job? ______________________.

1.2 What is more important for choosing a job, passion or skill?

The Power of Passion

Many people ask, "What is the best job?" The answer is often the job you love. We call this passion. When you have passion, work is not just work. It feels like fun! Passion is important because it gives you energy. If you love your job, you will not get tired easily. You will want to learn more. This helps you get better every day. This is called sustainable growth. It means your skills and happiness keep getting bigger over a long time.

For example, a person who loves cooking does not see work as boring. They read about food and try new recipes. This passion helps them grow from a simple cook into a great chef. Choosing a job you love is key to a long and happy career.

The Power of Skill

Some people choose a job not because of love, but because of skill. If you are good at something, you can find success. It is possible to learn to love a job. Maybe you are great with computers, but you don't love them. You take a job as a programmer. In the first few weeks, the job is hard. But because you have the skill, you learn fast. When you finish a difficult task, you feel proud. This pride and success can grow. You don't need passion to start a job, but skill can help you finish well and feel satisfied. Your natural ability makes the work easy, and easy work is happy work!

1.3 Fill-in-the-Blank Sentence

Use the words in the box to fill in the blanks.

apply	boss	experience	colleague	advertisement
workplace	part-time	opening	unemployed	salary

1 The new job has a very good ______________.

2 My ______________ gives me work to do every day.

3 The office is a very noisy ______________.

4 I will ______________ for three jobs this week.

5 There is one job ______________ for a new cook at the restaurant.

6 She has a ______________ job and only works on Saturdays.

7 A ______________ is a person you work with.

8 I have five years of ______________ as a waiter.

9 I saw the job ______________ in the newspaper.

10 He is ______________ now, but he is looking for a job.

1.4 Sentences with Vocabulary

Use the words on the left in a new sentence. This will help you use the word again later.

1	experience	I don't have the experience needed for this position yet.
2	apply	
3	workplace	
4	advertisement	
5	opening	

1.5 Sample Advertisements

Read about the positions in the job advertisements. Then answer the comprehension questions.

A. Job Advertisement: Junior Software Developer (Full-Time)

Company: Innovate Solutions Group (ISG)

Location: Tech Hub Building, City Centre, Manchester, UK

Are you a highly motivated and talented recent graduate looking for a rewarding entry-level position? Innovate Solutions Group is searching for a Junior Software Developer to join our dynamic and growing Development Team. This is a full-time, permanent opportunity to kick-start your career in technology. We offer flexible hours, a competitive starting salary, and excellent benefits.

Key Responsibilities:

- **Code Development:** Write clean, efficient, and well-documented code in Java and Python.
- **Team Collaboration:** Work closely with Senior Developers and the Project Manager to understand project goals and deadlines. This involves daily team meetings.
- **Testing and Debugging:** Perform unit testing and troubleshoot software problems.
- **Maintenance:** Assist with the maintenance and updating of existing software systems.
- **Documentation:** Create and maintain technical documentation for all assigned projects.

Essential Skills and Qualifications:

- A bachelor's degree in Computer Science, Engineering, or a related field.
- Basic experience with object-oriented programming.
- Knowledge of databases, especially SQL.
- Strong problem-solving skills and a proactive attitude.
- Excellent communication skills for reporting progress to the team.

How to Apply: Send your latest résumé and a professional cover letter detailing your experience with coding projects to careers@innovatesg.co.uk. We look forward to reviewing your application!

Comprehension Questions

1 What is the main programming language used? ____________________.

2 What education is required for this job? ____________________.

3 What specific type of testing will the developer do? ____________________.

4 If a developer has a problem, what must they do? ____________________.

5 What skills are needed? ____________________.

B. Job Advertisement: English Language Instructor

Academy: Global Learners Language Academy (GLLA)

Location: Gangnam District, Seoul, South Korea (near subway station)

Global Learners Language Academy is a reputable, modern private language school seeking a highly enthusiastic and dedicated English Language Instructor to teach young learners (ages 6–12). This is an exciting opportunity for English speakers to gain valuable teaching experience in a welcoming environment. We offer a generous monthly salary and housing stipend.

Schedule and Environment:

- **Contract:** 12 months, renewable.
- **Working Hours:** Monday to Friday, 2:00 PM to 9:00 PM (evenings).
- **Curriculum:** Prepared curriculum and materials are provided; no lesson planning required.
- **Class Size:** Maximum of 12 students per class.

Required Qualifications (What you need):

- A bachelor's degree in any subject.
- A recognized TEFL, TESOL, or CELTA certification (minimum 100 hours).
- Ability to manage a lively classroom and use positive classroom management techniques.

Benefits Package:

- Competitive monthly wage (KRW 2.5 million–2.8 million).
- Monthly housing allowance.
- National health insurance and pension enrollment.
- 10 days of paid vacation time, plus all national holidays.

To Apply: Email your résumé and a recent photo to recruiting@globalacademy.com. Please include the names and contact details of two references.

Comprehension Questions

1 What age group will the teacher be teaching? ______________________.

2 What teaching certificates are mentioned? ______________________.

3 What does the academy offer to help with rent? ______________________.

4 How much lesson planning is required? ______________________.

5 What is the required length of the first contract? ______________________.

1.6 Gap Fill A

With a partner choose one person to use Gap Fill A. Your partner will use Gap Fill B (in the back of the book). Practice the conversation with a partner and write the missing information in the blanks.

A I saw a new job advert yesterday. I think I will apply for it.

B Oh, nice! Is it a full-time ______________ ?

A Yes. It's a good step up. I've been unemployed for too long.

B I know that feeling! Did they say what the ______________ is?

A They listed a good range. It's better than my previous job.

B That's good news. What kind of ______________ are they looking for?

A They want experience in customer service, which I have a lot of.

B Perfect. I hope the new ______________ is nice, though.

A Me too. My last one was terrible!

B And you need a friendly ______________ to work with, right?

A Absolutely! I just want a better workplace than before.

B I understand. Are you applying for a full-time or a ______________ job?

A Full-time. I need the hours.

B Well, I hope you get an interview soon!

A Thanks! I'm sending the application now.

B Good luck!

1.7 Job Fit

Find a position that you would like to apply for. Answer the questions to help you choose. Use the checklist to make sure you have all the information you need to proceed.

1 Do I understand the work? Can I explain the responsibilities to a friend in my own language?

2 Can I do this job now? Do I have at least three skills from the requirements section?

3 Is the pay/time good for my life? Do the salary and the working hours fit my current needs?

4 Will I feel happy here? Based on the location and the job description, do I think the workplace culture will be friendly or stressful?

5 Is this job a good next step? Will this job teach me new skills or give me experience that helps me reach my dream job in the future?

1.8 Task Checklist

Use the classified ads on the next page to choose a job. You will use the information you find to help you write your résumé and cover letter. This will also be the job that you use for the interview. If you do not like the jobs in the classified ads, look online.

☐	Job Title Match	I understand exactly what the position is.
☐	Location	The workplace location is good for me (e.g., easy travel).
☐	My Skills (3+)	I have three or more of the required skills or qualifications.
☐	Education/Certificates	I have the necessary degree or certificate listed.
☐	Work Hours	The working hours and days are acceptable.
☐	Starting Date	I am available to start work on the required date.
☐	Experience Needed	I meet the minimum level of experience.
☐	Required Documents	I have all the documents ready.
☐	Application Method	I know how to apply (email, website form, phone call).
☐	Application Deadline	I will apply before the deadline.

1.9 Classified Ads

Look at the advertisements for jobs. Think about what job you want.

Marketing Assistant

Join our creative team! Help with social media and campaigns. Good communication is a must for this entry-level position. Send CV to marketing@company.kor

IT Support Specialist

Solve tech problems. Provide technical support to staff. Basic computer skill and problem-solving required. Send CV to Mr. Kim at ITSUpport@ company.co.kr

Junior Accountant

Grow your accounting career. Assist with daily financial records. Attention to detail is key for this full-time opening. Email: jobs@financeco.kor

HR Administrator

Manage employee records and office tasks. Strong organization skills and a friendly attitude required. Contact: Email HR: apply@ hrsolutions.kor

Creative Content Creator

Produce videos and text for social media. Must be enthusiastic about new ideas. Contact: Portfolio to create@media.kor

Sales Opportunity!

Meet clients, grow sales. Find new customers and build relationships. Good communication skills and a positive attitude are important. Email HR: apply@salesathon.ko

Research Assistant

Help us discover new things! Collect and analyze data for projects. Good at finding information and writing short reports. Contact: Email: research@lab.kor

Executive Secretary Role

Support our senior manager. Manage schedules and prepare documents. Excellent organizational skill and punctual attendance required. Contact: Send résumé to exec.jobs@ globalcorp.kor

Future Engineer Wanted

Design and build with us. Work on new product development. Basic engineering skill and strong problem-solving needed. Contact: Email CV to eng.careers@firm.kor

1.10 Unit Task Options

Option A:

Find a job in the advertisements above to help you apply for a real position. This will support your documents and help you with your interview.

Option B:

Find a job advertisement online. Your teacher will share some common websites with you in class. Find a real job advertisement online for which you would like to apply. Use the questions below to evaluate the job and write important information. You will be able to use this throughout our class. Having a real reference will give you a target for the résumé, cover letter, and interview.

Job Title : ____________________________.   Company :____________________________.

	Question	Answer
1	Do I understand the work?	
2	Is the workplace location good for me?	
3	Is the pay and working hours acceptable?	
4	Will this job teach me new skills?	
5	Will this job help me reach my dream job in the future?	
6	Do I understand exactly what the position is?	
7	Do I have the necessary degree or certificate?	
8	Do I have three or more of the required skills ?	
9	Do I meet the minimum level of experience requested?	
10	What is the hiring manager's contact information?	

UNIT 2 Write a Résumé

The résumé is a professional self-introduction document. The résumé, sometimes called a C.V., has a few different styles. We want to focus on a descriptive résumé that uses easy-to-read patterns. Managers like this style because it is quick and easy to read. Focus on highlighting value when writing your résumé.

UNIT 2 Goals

- Write a professional résumé that uses a descriptive, easy-to-read style.
- Structure the résumé using clear headers.
- Highlight valuable skills and accomplishments relevant to the desired job.
- Use reverse chronological order when listing education and experience, and ensure the page is fully utilized.

2.1. Discussion Questions

Discuss these questions with a partner. Write short keywords to help you remember your answers. Consider each question one at a time, answering each with your partner as you take notes.

1 What is the main purpose of a résumé? ______________________.

2 Should a résumé be long or short? ______________________.

3 What contact information do you need? ______________________.

4 How can you make a résumé easier to read? ______________________.

5 How can you highlight valuable information? ______________________.

2.2 The Importance of Experience

Clubs

Joining clubs shows employers that you are more likely to try new things and that you are curious. This is something that prospective employers look for when they are hiring. For some students, you may not have a lot of work experience. School clubs and volunteer work are less professional, but prove that you have a passion for the work.

Examples of your work

One way to make your development more trustworthy is to provide examples of your work. Consider the following examples of unpaid experience. Discuss with a partner what skills these show and how you could prove what you learned in each.

	Experience	Skills	Evidence
1	Creative Writing Club	Writing, editing, creativity	Links to blog posts
2	Astronomy Club		
3	Beach Clean-up Volunteer		
4	Content Creator		

2.3 Fill-in-the-Blank Sentence

Use the words in the box to fill in the blanks.

photo	university	date	accomplishment	objective
manager	dear	enthusiastic	enclosed	sincerely

1 I wrote a short ________ about my best qualities at the top.

2 The ________ explains what job you want.

3 I need to write about my ________ jobs on the form.

4 Remember to write the ________ you started and finished your last job.

5 The ________ of winning the award was a big one for my career.

6 ________ names must be clearly listed under the Education section.

7 Your ________ information should be at the top of the résumé near your name.

8 Use a clear ________ for your résumé so it is easy for managers to read quickly.

9 If you speak multiple languages, list them under the ________ category on your résumé.

10 You do not need a ________ on your résumé. In some countries, it is illegal!

2.4 Sentences with Vocabulary

Use the words on the left in a new sentence. This will help you use the word again later.

1	bullet points	*You should list your skills under your experience in bullet points.*
2	header	
3	soft skills	
4	reverse chronological	
5	objective	

2.5 Résumé Standards

Read about the goals of the résumé below. Consider how you can write headers and how to increase the value of your information. Then answer the comprehension questions.

A. Good Résumé Headers

Your résumé should be customized to fit the job you are applying for. You should try to highlight your skills by putting your most appropriate experiences first. Placing these items at the top/middle of your résumé makes sure the manager reads them first. Experience and Education should be included in all résumés. After writing your name and contact information, you should get creative to completely fill one page. Consider the following and write some ideas for each possible header in your résumé.

Possible Headers

- **Profile:** Write 3-4 sentences about your achievements and your goals for the future.
- **Soft Skills:** Highlight some of your most useful soft skills.
- **Awards:** List some of your most pertinent awards.
- **Languages:** Highlight your ability to speak multiple languages and your level in each.

Résumé Standards

- **Do not lie:** Only use real information about things you have already done.
- **Write positive things only:** Do not include any negative information.
- **Fill the page:** Do not have any empty space.
- **Header:** The Header of the section should be bold and clear.
- **Reverse Chronological Order:** History is listed in reverse chronological order, starting with the most recent job.

Comprehension Questions

1 What should be written in the Profile header? ____________________.

2 What is not normally included on a résumé? ____________________.

3 In what order should you list work experience? ____________________.

4 What patterns should be in the résumé? ____________________.

5 What is one formatting standard for the headers? ____________________.

B. How can I describe my history clearly and professionally?

Your résumé history must use bullet points to make the information quick and easy to read. Under your Experience section, each bullet point should describe a valuable accomplishment, not just a daily task. Look at the example below.

Experience

Connect Communication Company

2025

Sales Representative

- Generated new revenue by identifying and securing 15 new corporate clients
- Cultivated strong client relationships through effective communication skills
- Developed and implemented efficient strategies for new customers

Do not include any negative information. Focus on what you achieved and what skills you used. For example, instead of writing "I worked with a team," write "I collaborated with five colleagues to solve a problem, showing teamwork skills." Using bullet points helps you highlight valuable skills and accomplishments relevant to the desired job.

To make your job history trustworthy, you must clearly write the official company names where you worked and the university names where you studied. This uses the prestige of the institution to make your words easier to trust. If you need to change languages, find the official English spelling. If the workplace is not clear, include an extra word to clarify.

It is also important to include your Job Title (e.g., "Team Leader" or "Math Teacher"). The job title is very valuable because it tells the manager your level of responsibility. Remember that your job history must always be listed in reverse chronological order, meaning the newest job is listed first.

Comprehension Questions

1 How can you build trust with your résumé? ______________________.

2 What should a bullet point describe? ______________________.

3 Why is the Job Title valuable on a résumé? ______________________.

4 In what order must you list your jobs? ______________________.

5 What is the purpose of using bullet points? ______________________.

2.6 Gap Fill A

With a partner choose one person to use Gap Fill A. Your partner will use Gap Fill B (in the back of the book). Practice the conversation with a partner and write the missing information in the blanks.

A My résumé needs work. Is this format okay?

B It looks neat. Let's check your _________ section first.

A I put the university graduation date there.

B Perfect. Now for the work _________ section.

A Yes. I listed all my previous job titles here.

B Good. And did you list your biggest _________ at your last job?

A Yes, I added that I saved the company money.

B Excellent. You must include a short _________ at the very top.

A I did! Below that, I wrote my career objective.

B Great. You clearly need to list your language _________.

A I said I speak English and Spanish.

B Fantastic. What about the people for your _________?

A I have three people. Do I put their contact details on the page?

B No, just say "__________________."

A Okay, that's better.

B It looks ready to send!

2.7 Goal Questions

Your assignment is to write a professional résumé that is ready to send to a manager. Use the questions below to help you prepare to write.

1 What headers should you choose to completely fill the page?

2 Where should you include bullet-point descriptions?

3 What are the most valuable skills the manager is looking for in your résumé and how can you make them easy to find?

4 What can you include to prove that you have skills?

5 What template can you use to make your résumé look professional and match the job you are applying for?

2.8 Task Checklist

Your assignment is to write a professional résumé that is ready to send to a manager. Make sure your résumé is organized and matches this job by completing the following tasks.

☐	Use Clear Headers	Use clear, bold headers for each section.
☐	Reverse Chronological Order	List work history and education starting with the latest job or degree first.
☐	Focus on Accomplishments	Use bullet points to describe accomplishments, not just daily tasks.
☐	Highlight Skills	Include valuable soft skills and technical skills relevant to the job.
☐	Ensure Contact Accuracy	Check that all contact information (phone, email) is correct.
☐	Include University/ Company Names	Use official university names and company names to make history trustworthy.
☐	Check Formatting Standards	Use the same font and color throughout the document.
☐	Avoid Negative Information	Do not include any negative information.
☐	Fill the Page	Use the space to fill the page without adding an extra page.
☐	Write a Profile or Objective	Include short sentences summarizing your history and/or goals.

2.9 Good and Bad Résumés

Look at the résumés below. Consider what is good and bad about both. Use the discussion questions to help you analyze them with a partner. Refer to the back of the book for possible answers to the questions.

Discussion Questions

1. Is this person good at graphic design? Why or why not?
2. What is wrong with the formatting?
3. Is the contact information good? What would you change?
4. How do you feel about the colors?
5. What do you think about the font?
6. Do you understand what skills he learned in school?
7. What would you change about the text size and font?
8. Is the skills section helpful?
9. How is the picture?
10. Any other problems?

Résumé A - Bad Example

Richard Sanchez
Graphic Designer

I'm a creative Graphic Designer with expertise in branding, digital design, and visual communication, passionate about delivering innovative solutions.

Contact
XXX-XXXX-XXXX
wastingtime@fmail.com
www.instagram.com
Seoul

Education
Rimberio University
Bachelor's Degree In Graphic Designer
2010 - 2014

Babbin High School
Graduate
2015 - 2017

Award
Rimberio Competition
First Logo Design | 2020
Rimberio Competition
First Logo Design 2020

Work Experience

Studio Shodwe (2014 - 2015)
Graphic Designer Internship
- Creating Visual Designs
- Collaborating with Teams

Liceria Company (2016 - 2021)
Junior Graphic Designer
- I created designs that were really good
- Revising and Editin

Borcelle Studios (2022 - 2024)
Senior Graphic Designer
- Leading Design Projects
- Mentoring Junior Designers

Skills
Design Software
UI/UX Design
Typography
Branding and Logo
Concept Development

Résumé B - Good Example

RICHARD SANCHEZ

MARKETING MANAGER

CONTACT

+123-456-7890

hello@reallygreatsite.com

www.reallygreatsite.com

SKILLS

- Project Management
- Public Relations
- Teamwork
- Time Management
- Leadership
- Effective Communication
- Critical Thinking
- Digital Marketing

LANGUAGES

- English (Fluent)
- French (Fluent)
- German (Basic)
- Spanish (Intermediate)

ACHIEVEMENTS

- Salesman of the month
- Project Leader
- Blog writer
- Conference presenter

PROFILE

I am a motivated marketing manager with over ten years of experience. I am a proven leader, focusing on developing talent and communicating freely and often with my team. I have experience managing brand image and public relations. I pride myself on my critical thinking and awareness. I also hold an M.A. and B.A. in Management from Wardlere University. I am motivated to work with other passionate, creative minds.

WORK EXPERIENCE

Borcelle Studio 2020- PRESENT
Marketing Manager & Specialist

- Develop and execute comprehensive marketing strategies and campaigns that align with the company's goals and objectives.
- Lead, mentor, and manage a high-performing marketing team, fostering a collaborative and results-driven work environment.
- Monitor brand consistency across marketing channels and materials.

Fauget Studio 2012 - 22019
Marketing Manager & Specialist

- Create and manage the marketing budget, ensuring efficient allocation of resources and optimizing ROI.
- Oversee market research to identify emerging trends, customer needs, and competitor strategies.

Studio Shodwe 2011 - 2012
Marketing Manager & Specialist

- Develop and maintain strong relationships with partners, agencies, and vendors to support marketing initiatives.
- Monitor and maintain brand consistency across all marketing channels and materials.

EDUCATION

Master of Business Management 2029 - 2031
School of business | Wardiere University
GPA: 3.8 / 4.0

Bachelor of Business Management 2025 - 2029
School of business | Wardiere University
GPA: 3.8 / 4.0

Discussion Questions

1. Do you think this person is professional?
2. What is good about the formatting?
3. Is the contact information good? What would you change?
4. How do you feel about the colors?
5. What do you think about the font?
6. Do you understand what skills he learned in school?
7. Is it easy to read and find information?
8. Is the skills section helpful? How is it consistent with the information in the other parts?
9. Do you think it should have a picture?
10. Any other comments?

2.10 Unit Task

Write a professional résumé. Structure the résumé using clear headers like:

- Profile
- Education
- Experience

Choose more that match your history to the job expectations in order to fill the page.

UNIT 3 Write a Cover Letter

A cover letter is a formal email you send with your résumé. It is your chance to introduce yourself to the manager. You must use polite and formal language to make a good first impression and show that you are serious about the job.

UNIT 3 Goals

- Write a formal cover letter.
- Use polite language.
- Show your best experience and skills.
- Structure an effective business email.

3.1 Discussion Questions

Discuss these questions with a partner. Write short keywords to help you remember your answers. Consider each question one at a time, answering each with your partner as you take notes.

1 What is the goal of a cover letter? ______________________________.

2 Is informal language good in a cover letter? ______________________________.

3 Do you need to know the manager's name? ______________________________.

4 What skills should you add to a cover letter? ______________________________.

5 How do you finish a professional letter? ______________________________.

3.2 Writing Professionally

Formal Etiquette is Key

A cover letter must use formal language from beginning to end. This shows the manager that you understand professional etiquette (polite rules). The tone is important for a business letter. You must use a formal greeting like "Dear Mr. Smith" and a formal closing like "sincerely." If you use casual or informal words, the manager might think you are not serious about the position. Keeping the style very formal helps you make a positive first impression.

First Impression

The content of your cover letter is where you show the manager who you are and make your first impression as a serious candidate. This is your chance to describe your best experience and skills. You should write clearly about the specific position you want in the first line of the opening paragraph. You must be enthusiastic about the job, but still professional. Your goal is to use the strongest facts from your résumé. You will attach that file to the bottom of the cover letter email. You want to encourage the manager to call you for an interview.

3.3 Fill-in-the-Blank Sentence

Use the words in the box to fill in the blanks.

formal	greeting	opening	position	closing
manager	dear	enthusiastic	enclosed	sincerely

1 You must start your letter with "______________ Mr. Smith."

2 My résumé is ______________ with this letter.

3 I finished the letter with "______________," before my name.

4 A business letter should use ______________ language, not slang.

5 I am writing to apply for the sales ______________.

6 The "Dear Sir or Madam" part is called the ______________.

7 The first paragraph is the letter's ______________.

8 I feel very ______________ about the chance to work for your company.

9 The final paragraph is the ______________ where you ask for an interview.

10 I sent the letter to the Hiring ______________.

3.4 Sentences with Vocabulary

Use the words on the left in a new sentence. This will help you use the word again later.

1	etiquette	Cover letters are an email that show your polite, formal etiquette.
2	impression	
3	polite	
4	rude	
5	describe	

3.5 Cover Letter Standards

Read about the goals of the cover letter below. Consider how you can structure your document to highlight your professionalism and make a positive first impression. Then answer the comprehension questions.

A. Formal Etiquette and Structure

A cover letter is a formal email you send with your résumé. Its primary function is to introduce yourself and show that you are serious about the job by using polite and formal language. The style must remain formal from beginning to end to show the manager that you understand professional etiquette. You must use a formal greeting, like "Dear Mr. Smith," and a formal closing, like "Sincerely."

The letter should be structured clearly. In the opening paragraph, you must clearly state the specific position you want in the first line. The content must be enthusiastic but professional. Your goal is to make a positive first impression.

If you use casual or informal words, the manager might think you are not serious about the position. Keeping the style very formal helps you make a positive first impression.

Considerations for Formal Structure

- Use a formal greeting.
- The first line of the opening must clearly state the specific position you want.
- The tone must be enthusiastic but professional.
- Use a formal closing before your name.
- Check for professional etiquette.

Comprehension Questions

1. Why is maintaining a formal style so important? ______________________.
2. How should you greet the manager? ______________________.
3. Why write the position on the first line? ______________________.
4. Why would informal words be inappropriate? ______________________.
5. What should you write at the end? ______________________.

B. Content, Skills, and First Impressions

The content of your cover letter is where you describe your best experience and skills. The cover letter is your chance to use the strongest facts from your résumé, which should be an attachment. The goal is to use this content to encourage the manager to call you for an interview. This will only happen if they immediately consider your writing professional. The cover letter is successful if it is professional enough to make the manager want to open your résumé and consider you for the position.

You must ensure the communication follows proper business email structure. This includes using an appropriate subject line and clearly including your personal contact information in the signature area. Remember that the cover letter is a key part of the hiring process. There are specific rules to consider in order to make yourself seem like the best person for the job. By structuring an effective business email and describing your relevant experience, you will make a positive first impression and show your skills.

Considerations for Content and Impression

- Describe your best experience and skills.
- Keep your cover letter short and professional.
- Write your name in the subject line of the email and the position.
- Include personal contact information in the signature area.
- Your goal is to use strong facts to make a positive first impression and encourage an interview.

Comprehension Questions

1 What is the goal of the cover letter? ____________________.

2 What are your best skills and experiences? ____________________.

3 Why is the subject line of the email important? ____________________.

4 How long should the cover letter be? ____________________.

5 What verbs can you use to show strong facts? ____________________.

3.6 Gap Fill A

With a partner choose one person to use Gap Fill A. Your partner will use Gap Fill B (in the back of the book). Practice the conversation with a partner and write the missing information in the blanks.

A I'm writing the cover letter now. I'll start with the proper greeting.

B Good. Remember to write "______________ Mr. Smith," not "Hello."

A Right. I must keep the whole style very formal.

B Exactly. The tone is important for a business letter.

A My opening explains why I am enthusiastic about the job.

B That's great! Enthusiasm helps.

A I clearly wrote the job position I want in the first line.

B Smart. Did you mention that your résumé is ______________ ?

A Yes, I did. I hope the hiring manager reads it soon.

B Me too. What are you writing for the final ______________ ?

A I plan to use the word "Sincerely."

B That is the correct formal word to use.

A I also added a sentence about waiting for their call.

B Perfect. It sounds professional.

A Thanks for checking!

B No problem.

3.7 Goal Questions

Find a position that you like. Answer the questions to help you choose. Use the checklist to make sure you have all the information you need to proceed.

1. How should you greet a manager at the beginning of the email?
2. How do you make a clear email subject that managers can find again?
3. What formal word must be used for the final closing?
4. What are your best skills from your résumé that you can describe to the manager?
5. Why is it important to sound enthusiastic about the job?

3.8 Task Checklist

Your assignment is to write a formal cover letter introducing yourself to the hiring manager of the job you want. Use appropriate formal language and etiquette for greetings and closings. Use experience and skills from the résumé to make a positive impression. Structure an effective business email including an opening, a closing, and a clear position statement.

☐	Use Formal Language	Use formal language and maintain a professional tone throughout the letter.
☐	Write an Appropriate Subject	Include an appropriate subject line (avoiding casual language like "Hey there!").
☐	Use Formal Greeting	Start the letter with a proper greeting (e.g., "Dear Mrs. Smith").
☐	State Position Clearly	The first line of the opening clearly states the specific position.
☐	Mention Résumé Enclosed	Include a sentence that your résumé is attached.
☐	Show Enthusiasm	Show that you are enthusiastic and serious about the job opportunity.
☐	Include Experience/Skills	Include 3 examples of experience/skills to make a good first impression.
☐	Write a Professional Closing	Finish the letter with a formal closing (e.g., "Sincerely").
☐	Check Etiquette	Check for professional etiquette.
☐	Include Personal Information	Include personal contact information in the signature area.

3.9 Good and Bad Cover Letters

Look at the cover letters below. Consider what is good and bad about both. Use the discussion questions to help you analyze them with a partner. Refer to the back of the book for possible answers to the questions.

Cover Letter A - Bad Example

COVER LETTER

Dear Hiring Manager,

Hi there! I am a student in University. I am ready to work with you! I am confident in my ability to contribute meaningfully to your team. I have the skills you are looking for because I am passionate about my work and I am never late.

In my previous role, I led a project that improved team efficiency a lot. I worked part-time at 2 different jobs last summer, so I am good at communication and teamwork.

Though I am just a student, I do not think that is a weakness because I work hard and I come to work everyday with a smile. :)

You will not regret picking me. I am the best.

Bye,

Rhonda Readie

Discussion Questions

1 What should be written at the top of a cover letter?

2 What is wrong with the greeting?

3 Do you like the image at the bottom?

4 How do you feel about the colors?

5 Does this look formal?

6 Do you think their experience is valuable?

7 How would you change the first sentence?

8 What is the biggest problem with this cover letter?

9 Why is the sentence "You will not regret picking me" so inappropriate?

10 How would you change the closing?

Cover Letter B - Good Example

ANNA MUTIARA
Specialist Journalist

+123-456-7890 hello@reallygreatsite.com 123 Anywhere St., Any City

17 June, 2025

JOHAN SAMUDRA
Manager Wardiere Inc.
123 Anywhere St., Any City

Recruitment Journalist

Dear Mr. Johan,

I am excited to apply for the position of junior journalist. I have experience writing on my own blog where I have been covering trends in cosmetics and fashion for the past two years. I am currently studying journalism at the University of Jean. There I have learned to write polished work and edit consistently even if I think it is perfect.

I believe I will be an asset to your company and I would love to speak with you more about the position. Thank you very much for your time.

Sincerely,

Anna Mutiara

Discussion Questions

1. Do you think this looks professional?
2. Will you use the same contact information?
3. Is the greeting appropriate?
4. What is the right way to start your email content?
5. Do you believe that their experience is real?
6. Can you easily find their skills?
7. Is this a good length?
8. Do you think their skills match the position?
9. What parts of this will you use as good examples for your cover letter?
10. Do you think they should have written anything more?

3.10 Unit Task

Write a formal cover letter to accompany your résumé. Use appropriate formal language and etiquette for greetings and closings. Use experience and skills from the résumé to make a positive impression. Structure an effective business email including an opening, a closing, and a clear position statement.

UNIT 4 Prepare for a Job Interview

This unit helps you get ready for the job interview. Preparation is very important! We will learn how to anticipate and answer common questions. You will also practice using good body language and professional dress, so you look reliable and confident.

UNIT 4 Goals

- Learn common interview questions.
- Practice your answers without a script.
- Use good body language.
- Research the company before the interview.

4.1. Discussion Questions

Discuss these questions with a partner. Write short keywords to help you remember your answers. Consider each question one at a time, answering each with your partner as you take notes.

1 What should you do before an interview? ____________________.

2 What are common interview questions? ____________________.

3 How can you speak confidently? ____________________.

4 What makes you feel nervous? ____________________.

5 Should you speak fast or slow? ____________________.

4.2 Preparing for an Interview

Practicing Your Answers

The interview is about how you speak as well as what you say. It is important to practice your answers many times at home so you can speak clearly and confidently. You must research the company before the interview so you know what they do. When the interviewer asks a question, your answers should focus on your greatest strengths. Present yourself as a professional by not wasting any time. Quickly include keywords that you wrote in your résumé to answer the manager's primary questions.

Body Language and Presentation

Body language is just as important as the words you say. You should dress in professional clothes for the interview. It is essential to be punctual and arrive on time. When you meet the interviewer, give them a firm handshake. Sitting up straight and smiling are examples of good body language. Appropriate gestures help you communicate without using too many words.

4.3 Fill-in-the-Blank Sentence

Use the words in the box to fill in the blanks.

punctual	dress	firm	research	answer
practice	weakness	body language	question	strength

1 I hope the interviewer does not ask a difficult ____________ .

2 You must ____________ all the questions clearly.

3 I told the boss my biggest ____________ is that I work too slowly sometimes.

4 Being good at computers is my biggest ____________ .

5 It is important to be ____________ and arrive on time.

6 You should ____________ the company before your interview.

7 I need to ____________ in smart clothes for the meeting.

8 Good ____________ means sitting up straight and smiling.

9 Give the interviewer a ____________ handshake.

10 I will ____________ my answers at home many times.

4.4 Sentences with Vocabulary

Use the words on the left in a new sentence. This will help you use the word again later.

1	gesture	Gestures help you communicate without using too many words.
2	evidence	
3	adjectives	
4	clarification	
5	awkward	

4.5 Interview Preparation Standards

Read about what and how you should present yourself in a job interview below. Answer the questions to check for understanding.

A. Research, Content, and Confidence

Preparation is very important for the job interview. To ensure your answers are relevant, you must research the company before the interview so you know what they do. This research shows the manager you are serious about the position.

The interview is about how you speak as well as what you say. You must practice your answers many times at home so you can speak clearly and confidently. You should quickly include keywords that you wrote in your résumé to answer the manager's primary questions. You should prepare an answer to highlight your greatest strengths and a professional example of experience to support that strength.

You must practice speaking without a script to show genuine confidence. Presenting yourself as a professional by not wasting any time ensures you meet the unit goal of looking reliable and confident.

Considerations for Content and Confidence

- Research the company's latest news before the interview.
- Practice answers many times to speak clearly and confidently.
- Use keywords from your résumé to answer questions quickly.
- Identify your greatest strength and prepare professional experience to support it.
- Avoid reading from a script while practicing.

Comprehension Questions

1 What should you research before an interview? ______________________.

2 Why are keywords more helpful than stories? ______________________.

3 Should you memorize a script for an interview? ______________________.

4 Why is it important to highlight your strengths? ______________________.

5 Why are examples so important in an interview? ______________________.

B. Presentation and Body Language

Body language is just as important as the words you say. Your physical presentation is the second key area of preparation. You should dress in professional clothes for the interview. It is essential to be punctual and arrive on time (for example, 10 minutes early).

When you meet the interviewer, give them a firm handshake. Sitting up straight, smiling, and using appropriate gestures are examples of good body language. These details communicate without using too many words.

It is also good practice to prepare two physical items to bring with you: copies of your Résumé and Cover Letter. Your overall presentation—from your dress and punctuality to your firm handshake and posture—is crucial for making the interviewer perceive you as reliable and professional. Don't forget to write a thank-you email to the manager after the interview.

Considerations for Presentation and Body Language

- Dress in professional clothes.
- Be punctual (arrive on time, e.g., 10 minutes early).
- Give the interviewer a firm handshake.
- Use good body language (e.g., sitting up straight, smiling).
- Bring copies of your Résumé and Cover Letter.

Comprehension Questions

1 Why is it important to be on time? ______________________.

2 What message does a firm handshake send? ______________________.

3 Why is it important to use appropriate gestures? ______________________.

4 How does your appearance show professionalism? ______________________.

5 What should you do after the interview? ______________________.

4.6 Gap Fill A

With a partner choose one person to use Gap Fill A. Your partner will use Gap Fill B (in the back of the book). Practice the conversation with a partner and write the missing information in the blanks.

A I'm so scared about the job interview today.

B Don't be! You just need to be ________ . Arrive 10 minutes early.

A I will. I also need to remember to dress smartly.

B Yes, professional clothes are a must.

A I spent an hour yesterday trying to answer their common questions.

B Good. Did you ________ the company's latest news?

A Yes, I read everything on their website.

B Perfect. What did you decide to say is your biggest ________ ?

A I'll say I'm great at solving problems.

B Excellent. And how will you explain your ________ ?

A I'll say I work too hard, but I am learning to rest.

B That's a good answer. Remember to ________ a ________ handshake.

A I will. And I'll smile to show good body language.

B You've got this!

4.7 Goal Questions

Find a position that you like. Answer the questions to help you choose. Use the checklist to make sure you have all the information you need to proceed.

1. How should you practice answers so you do not read from a script?
2. What is one important thing you must research about the company?
3. How can you use body language to show you are confident, not awkward?
4. What physical item should you bring to the interview?
5. What is the function of asking about your greatest strength?

4.8 Task Checklist

Your assignment is to practice answering common interview questions to prepare for your job interview test. Practice appropriate body language and gestures. Research the company and the position to prepare before the interview. Remember that you need to practice speaking. Job interviews are about how you speak as well as what you say.

☐	Research the Company	Research the company's latest news on their website.
☐	Practice Answers	Practice answering common questions (e.g., introducing yourself) without memorizing a script.
☐	Identify Strength/Weakness	Prepare an answer to highlight your greatest strength and a professional example of experience.
☐	Be Punctual	Be punctual and arrive on time (e.g., 10 minutes early).
☐	Dress Appropriately	Dress in appropriate clothing for the interview.
☐	Practice Body Language	Practice using good body language (e.g., sitting comfortably and smiling).
☐	Perform Firm Handshake	I practiced giving a firm handshake.
☐	Prepare Interviewer Questions	I prepared questions to ask the interviewer at the end of the meeting.
☐	Bring Necessary Documents	I brought copies of my résumé and cover letter.
☐	Prepare Thank You Email	Plan to send a thank-you email after the interview.

4.9 Good and Bad Data

Look at the two examples of data. How would you analyze them? Consider the questions with your partner. This Smart Watch Company is trying to make a new design. Why is this data insufficient? Why is the Data in Example B more likely to help the company sell more watches?

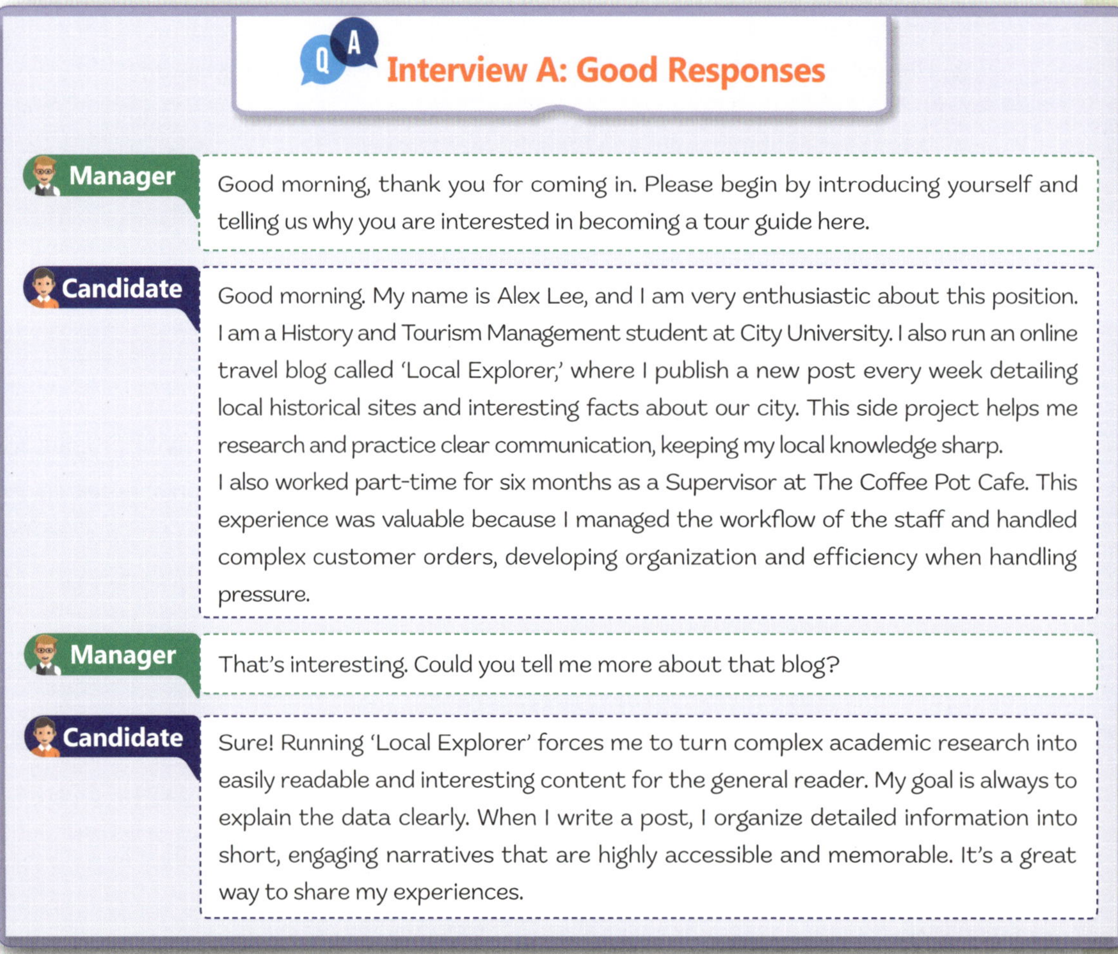

Interview A: Good Responses

Manager Good morning, thank you for coming in. Please begin by introducing yourself and telling us why you are interested in becoming a tour guide here.

Candidate Good morning. My name is Alex Lee, and I am very enthusiastic about this position. I am a History and Tourism Management student at City University. I also run an online travel blog called 'Local Explorer,' where I publish a new post every week detailing local historical sites and interesting facts about our city. This side project helps me research and practice clear communication, keeping my local knowledge sharp.
I also worked part-time for six months as a Supervisor at The Coffee Pot Cafe. This experience was valuable because I managed the workflow of the staff and handled complex customer orders, developing organization and efficiency when handling pressure.

Manager That's interesting. Could you tell me more about that blog?

Candidate Sure! Running 'Local Explorer' forces me to turn complex academic research into easily readable and interesting content for the general reader. My goal is always to explain the data clearly. When I write a post, I organize detailed information into short, engaging narratives that are highly accessible and memorable. It's a great way to share my experiences.

Discussion Questions

1 What valuable information is included in the first response?

2 Does all the candidate's experience match the position? Is this a problem?

3 What skills does the candidate describe? Do they fit the position?

4 How does the candidate start their responses? Is there a formula to follow?

5 How does the introduction change the focus of the second question?

Look at the conversation below. This candidate is applying for an accounting job. Look at the common errors made in the responses and discuss the questions with a partner.

Interview B: Bad Responses

Manager Good morning. Thank you for being punctual. Please begin by introducing yourself and telling us why you are interested in this Junior Accountant position.

Candidate Hey! I'm Jamie, and I'm super excited to be here. Honestly, I'm just a really passionate person, you know? I've got this great, positive attitude, and I love working with numbers. I think numbers are just fascinating! I've been doing some work with money things before, like helping out some friends and just generally enjoying the whole process. I know I could bring a really cool energy to your team because I'm very easy to get along with. I'm just ready to start my career now because I love accounting so much!

Manager Thank you. Now, what do you consider to be your greatest strength, and what is your greatest weakness?

Candidate That's a great question. My biggest strength is definitely being super helpful. I'm great at solving problems if anyone asks me.
I'd say my weakness is that I'm a perfectionist. I just can't stand mistakes. Sometimes, this means I spend too much time checking everything and working too much. To fix this, I'm trying to rely more on my coworkers, trusting them to check their own calculations, and making sure I organize my tasks better to manage my time efficiently. I still want everything to be perfect, but I'm learning to let small things pass so I can be more relaxed.

Discussion Questions

1 What do you think of the introduction?

2 Why do you think the manager asks such a general follow-up question?

3 Do you believe being helpful is a great strength? Why is this answer problematic here?

4 Why would a manager ask about your greatest weakness? What is the manager's objective?

5 If you were the manager, would you select this candidate for the position? Why or why not?

4.10 Unit Task

Practice answering common interview questions to prepare for your test. Practice appropriate body language and gestures. Research the company and prepare the necessary documents before the interview. Remember that you need to practice speaking. Job interviews are about how you speak as well as what you say.

PART 2 Career Success

Planning a Project and Writing a Formal Report

Once you have a job, you may need to suggest new ideas to your manager. To receive approval, you may need to write a proposal, a formal written request to start a new project. You must explain the main problem with a clear structure, propose a solution, and show the project's benefits. If your plan includes a survey, you must develop hypotheses. After the project is finished, you must create a formal report.

Analyzing Information and Confident Presentations

Before writing the report, you must analyze the collected data from your survey. You need to collect the data, look at the results, and identify trends. Presenting your findings is an important skill to practice so that you can connect and engage with the audience.

UNIT 5 Proposals

Once you have a job, you may need to suggest new ideas to your manager. A proposal is a formal document or request to begin a new project. We will learn how to structure a plan that convinces your manager that your idea is good, including the goals, budget, and timeline.

UNIT 5 Goals

- Write a formal business proposal.
- Develop hypotheses for a survey.
- Convince the manager to approve the proposal.
- Describe how your project will improve the company.

5.1 Discussion Questions

Discuss these questions with a partner. Write short keywords to help you remember your answers. Consider each question one at a time, answering each with your partner as you take notes.

1 What is a proposal? ________________________.

2 Why is it important to have a good title? ________________________.

3 What do you most want readers to know? ________________________.

4 How can you convince people of your plan? ________________________.

5 What is a timeline in a project proposal? ________________________.

5.2 Effective Proposals

The Essential Structure

A proposal is a formal written request to start a project. The manager needs to see a clear structure before granting approval. The introduction must clearly explain the main problem you are addressing. The proposal must include a budget to show how much money is needed and a timeline to show when each part of the work will be finished. The main goal of the proposal is to find a solution to the problem.

Hypotheses and Convincing Benefits

To make a convincing argument, you need to show the project's benefits (the good points). You must be able to suggest how the project will solve the problem. If your proposal includes a survey, you must develop a hypothesis, which is your guess about what you will learn from the survey. Even if your hypothesis is wrong later, creating it helps show the manager that you have a clear strategy for achieving the desired outcome. Consider the hypotheses below and think about what survey questions could be added to a survey to test them.

1 Men will buy more "sporty" looking cosmetics, women will buy more "luxurious" cosmetics.

2 People who like camping will buy more items if they are small, washable, and perform multiple tasks.

3 Our amusement park can make more money if we have more air-conditioned resting places.

5.3 Fill-in-the-Blank Sentence

Use the words in the box to fill in the blanks.

project	budget	suggest	request	introduction
timeline	solution	goal	approval	benefits

1 I want to ______________ a new way to clean the office.

2 The ______________ shows how much money we need.

3 We need to find a ______________ to this problem.

4 The new building is a big ______________ for the company.

5 I will explain the ______________ (good points) of my idea.

6 We will ______________ one new computer for the office.

7 We need the boss's ______________ to start the plan.

8 The ______________ shows when each part of the work will finish.

9 The ______________ explains the main topic of the plan.

10 The ______________ of this plan is to save money.

5.4 Sentences with Vocabulary

Use the words on the left in a new sentence. This will help you use the word again later.

1	implicit	You should avoid implicit information in a proposal. Make everything clear.
2	explicit	
3	confidence	
4	context	
5	hypothesis	

5.5 Proposal Standards

Read about how to write a professional project proposal below then answer the comprehension questions.

A. Structure, Goals, and Approval

A proposal is a formal written request to start a new project. The manager needs to see a clear structure before granting approval. The purpose of this proposal is to show the manager how your survey will receive responses from customers that help develop your plan.

To ensure the manager grants approval, the proposal must include specific details about your logic for starting the project. You must include your hypotheses– the guesses you want to prove true, your survey questions and answers– to ensure your data will be discoverable, your plan for analyzing the data– to make it clear you know what you are doing. The structure should be clear and encourage the manager's approval.

The proposal's focus should always be clear and easy to understand. You must avoid implicit information and make everything explicit. The manager wants you to simply state valid reasons for taking the company in a new direction. Some companies value this sort of independent work, which is called Research & Development. This project will use logic to explore your strategy for improving the company.

Considerations for Structure and Approval

- Write a formal written request to begin the project.
- Describe your hypotheses to get the manager interested in your project.
- Write your survey questions and answers to get feedback from the manager.
- Show how you will test your hypotheses once you have collected the data.
- Summarize your plan in 1-2 sentences and describe how the project will improve the company.

Comprehension Questions

1 Why should you include your hypotheses? __________________.

2 How can you make your survey easy to complete? __________________.

3 Why is implicit information bad? __________________.

4 What key structural components should you have? __________________.

5 Where should you write the goals of the project? __________________.

B. Strategy and Hypothesis Development

To be convincing, the proposal must show the project's benefits. This demonstrates how the project will improve the company. You must keep your writing short and clear throughout the document. This is a business proposal. Managers will look to understand your idea from the beginning. Do not waste time by trying to write too much. The key is to clearly state your idea, the plan, and maintain focus on how you will be developing some part of the company. Time is money!

If your project includes a survey, you must develop a hypothesis, which is your guess about what you will learn from the survey. This hypothesis should be a supposition that could be true but is not a well-known fact. Developing hypotheses helps show the manager that you have a clear strategy.

You must outline your plan for analyzing the data. Even if your hypothesis is proven false later, creating it helps show the manager you have a clear strategy for achieving the desired outcome, and documenting why it was false is part of the final plan.

Considerations for Strategy and Hypotheses

- Develop hypotheses (guesses) about what the survey will find.
- Show the project's benefits (the good points) to make a convincing argument.
- The hypotheses should not be facts.
- Include a plan for analyzing the data (survey responses).
- Use a clear strategy to create a convincing argument.

Comprehension Questions

1 Why is a hypothesis not a fact? ______________________________.

2 How can you preview your analysis strategy? ______________________________.

3 How can you describe your development plan? ______________________________.

4 Is it bad if your hypothesis is false? ______________________________.

5 What do you need to say about your survey? ______________________________.

5.6 Gap Fill A

With a partner choose one person to use Gap Fill A. Your partner will use Gap Fill B (in the back of the book). Practice the conversation with a partner and write the missing information in the blanks.

A I finished the plan. I will suggest it to the board tomorrow.

B Great. You mean the new software ______________ ?

A Yes. The main goal is to find a solution to our slow system.

B That's important. How big is the ______________ ?

A It's a 3-month project. We need a large budget for new equipment.

B Okay. I hope you get their ______________ quickly.

A I need to show them the amazing benefits of the software.

B That's right. What about the ______________ ?

A I included one that shows every step by week.

B Excellent. Did you clearly state the ______________ for the money?

A Yes, it's at the end.

B And is there a good ______________ ?

A Yes, it clearly states the software problem.

B Perfect. They will love it.

5.7 Goal Questions

Find a position that you would like to apply to. Answer the questions to help you choose. Use the checklist to make sure you have all the information you need to proceed.

1. What are some hypotheses about what the survey will find?
2. What is the main problem your proposal is trying to solve?
3. What are the benefits of this project for the company?
4. What survey questions would be good for identifying groups of people?
5. What answers to those questions should be expected?

5.8 Task Checklist

Your assignment is to write your project proposal with your group. Develop hypotheses for a survey that will find customer opinions that help the company. Convince the manager to grant project approval based on your proposal. Include:

1. An introduction describing the survey and how your data will improve the company.
2. Your survey questions and answers.
3. Your plan for analyzing the data.
4. A conclusion paragraph describing how you will use the data.

☐	Write Formal Request	I wrote a formal written proposal to begin a project.
☐	Include Introduction/Problem	Clearly explain the main problem in the introduction.
☐	Define Goal and Solution	Define the main goal and propose a definitive solution.
☐	Develop Hypotheses	Develop hypotheses about what the survey will find.
☐	Outline Benefits	Show the benefits of the project to convince the manager.
☐	Include Clear Questions	Write simple survey questions that identify group opinions.
☐	Multiple Choice Answers	Write answers to questions that target options you want.
☐	Seek Approval	Structure the document to encourage the manager's approval.
☐	Include a Plan for Data	Show how you will analyze the survey responses.
☐	Write Convincing Argument	Use a clear strategy to create a convincing argument.

5.9 Good and Bad Survey Questions

Look at the questions and answers below. This group is trying to sell meal kits to university students on campus. Consider the value of their questions and answers and how they will be able to design a marketing campaign.

Survey A: Good Example

1 How important is having passion for your daily job tasks?

① Not Important ② ③ ④ ⑤ Very Important

2 I would accept a starting salary 10% below average if it was my dream job.

① Strongly Disagree ② ③ ④ ⑤ Strongly Agree

3 Have you joined a university club or participated in volunteer work while at school?

Ⓐ Yes Ⓑ No

4 I feel confident in my ability to find a valuable job immediately after graduation.

① Strongly Disagree ② ③ ④ ⑤ Strongly Agree

Hypothesis 1: Students who value passion will accept a lower salary.

Hypothesis 2: Students who have experience in university clubs or volunteer work feel more confident about their career prospects.

Hypothesis Testing Process
1. Question 1 (High-4,5) Question 2 (High-4,5)= True
2. Question 3 (Yes) Question 4 (High)= True

Discussion Questions

1 Why is this data easier to use?

2 What are variable questions and control questions in a survey?

3 How does using numbers (like a 1 to 5 scale) speed up the data analysis process?

4 What do you do if your hypothesis is false? Is this a bad thing? Does it change your goal?

5 What is the danger of assuming that correlation equals causation when analyzing your survey results?

Survey B: Bad Example

In this survey, students want to explore lifestyles, learning, and confidence. This survey will be used to make counseling services for students. Look at some of the problems and discuss.

1 How long do you usually sleep?

Ⓐ 0-6 hours Ⓑ 6-12 hours Ⓒ 12-18 hours Ⓓ 18-24 hours

2 I am comfortable with my English level.

① Strongly Agree ② ③ ④ ⑤ Strongly Disagree

3 I am satisfied with my major and I have a good idea of my future career.

① Strongly Disagree ② ③ ④ ⑤ Strongly Agree

4 I feel confident in my ability to find a valuable job immediately after graduation.

① Strongly Disagree ② ③ ④ ⑤ Strongly Agree

5 How many hours do you study outside of class per week?

Ⓐ 0 hours Ⓑ -2 hours Ⓒ 5 hours Ⓓ 10 hours Ⓔ +10 hours

Hypothesis 1: Students who are satisfied with their current major are confident of their future.

Hypothesis 2: Students who study more than 10 hours per week don't sleep well.

Discussion Questions

1 What are variable questions and control questions in a survey?

2 Why is it dangerous to assume that correlation equals causation?

3 What is wrong with the answer options in Question 1? How would you change them?

4 Why are the options in Question 2 problematic for this survey?

5 Why is a survey considered a success even if the initial hypothesis is proven false?

5.10 Unit Task

Write your project proposal with your group. Develop hypotheses for a survey that will help the company. Convince the manager to grant project approval based on your proposal. Include:

1 An introduction describing the survey and how your data will improve the company

2 Your survey questions and answers

3 Your plan for analyzing the data

4 A conclusion paragraph describing how you will use the data

UNIT 6 Analyzing Data

In this unit, we will learn how to look at information, or data. This information often comes from a survey that you conduct. We must collect the numbers, find trends, and use charts or graphs to understand what the results mean clearly.

UNIT 6 Goals

- Collect customer satisfaction information.
- Learn to read charts and graphs.
- Interpret trends and percentages in the results.
- Identify common mistakes in data analysis.

6.1 Discussion Questions

Discuss these questions with a partner. Write short keywords to help you remember your answers. Consider each question one at a time, answering each with your partner as you take notes.

1. What is "data"? ____________________.
2. Have you ever done a survey? ____________________.
3. Why is data important? ____________________.
4. Which is easier: a table or a picture? ____________________.
5. When do we use percentages? ____________________.

6.2 Readability

Collecting and Comparing Information

Data is simply information, usually facts and numbers. This information is often collected from a survey. After collecting the data, you need to look at the results and find a trend. It is important to compare the current data with previous results or other groups to see what has changed. The goal is to clearly understand customer satisfaction.

Visual Aids are Clearer

A large table full of raw numbers can be difficult for people to understand. This is why visual aids are used. A visual representation, like a chart or a graph (line graph), helps us see the data easily. You can use a percentage to show how much of the customer group chose a certain answer. The goal is to organize the information clearly so that managers can quickly find the necessary conclusions.

6.3 Fill-in-the-Blank Sentence

Use the words in the box to fill in the blanks.

graph	find	percentage	compare	result
collect	information	chart	trend	survey

1 We looked at all the ______________ about our customers.

2 The survey ______________ showed that 80% like the new product.

3 The ______________ helped us see the numbers in a picture.

4 The data shows a ______________ (way the numbers are going) for higher sales.

5 Only 20 ______________ of people chose the blue shirt.

6 We asked 100 people questions for our ______________ .

7 We need to ______________ the sales data from May and June.

8 What did you ______________ when you looked at the numbers?

9 We must ______________ all the test scores before we start.

10 The line ______________ went up very quickly in December.

6.4 Sentences with Vocabulary

Use the words on the left in a new sentence. This will help you use the word again later.

1	hierarchy	Present data in a clear list to show your logical hierarchy.
2	perspective	
3	resolution	
4	identify	
5	show	

6.5 Data Analysis Standards

Read about how to find results in your data below and check your understanding by answering the questions.

A. Collecting and Interpreting Results

Data is formally defined as information, typically facts and numbers. This information is most often collected from a survey designed to gather customer opinions or satisfaction metrics. After collecting the customer satisfaction information, you need to look at the results and identify trends.

The main goal of this stage is to interpret numerical results clearly to understand customer satisfaction. To make the data easy to analyze, you must ensure your survey response options are properly formatted: you should use numbers as much as possible (such as rating scales) and avoid short answers.

Furthermore, it is important to compare the current data with previous results or other customer groups to see what has changed. Organizing the data into variables (the main topics) and control questions (like age or location) helps streamline the analysis and allows for better comparison.

Considerations for Collection and Interpretation

- Collect customer satisfaction data.
- Look at the results and identify trends.
- Compare the data with previous results or other customer groups.
- Use numbers as much as possible (rating scales).
- Organize the data into variables and control questions.

Comprehension Questions

1 Why should you use numbers to analyze data? ______________________.

2 What does it mean to identify trends? ______________________.

3 Why is it important to make groups of responses? ______________________.

4 Why are short answers difficult to work with? ______________________.

5 Why are control questions helpful? ______________________.

B. Presentation and Analysis Errors

Once the numerical data has been interpreted and trends identified, you must present the findings clearly. A large table full of raw numbers can be difficult for managers to understand, so visual aids are necessary. Images, like a chart or a graph, should be used to organize the information. You can also use a percentage to show how much of the customer group chose a certain answer.

When analyzing the results, you must apply critical thinking. A fundamental warning in data analysis is that correlation does not equal causation! If two factors seem connected, you must avoid making false conclusions based only on related data.

Finally, your analysis must address the initial hypothesis. If your initial hypothesis was proven false, you must document why it was false, but do not delete it. This documentation is essential for transparency and for completing the overall project strategy, showing the manager exactly what you learned even when your guess was incorrect.

Considerations for Presentation and Errors

- Use visual aids like a chart or graph to explain data easily.
- Use a percentage to describe the results.
- Check to ensure correlation does not equal causation.
- If hypotheses are false, document why, but do not delete it.
- Present any surprising or interesting results clearly.

Comprehension Questions

1 Why are visual aids effective? ____________________.

2 Why does correlation not equal causation? ____________________.

3 When are percentages better than numbers? ____________________.

4 What if your hypothesis is false? ____________________.

5 When should you use graphs? ____________________.

6.6 Gap Fill A

With a partner choose one person to use Gap Fill A. Your partner will use Gap Fill B (in the back of the book). Practice the conversation with a partner and write the missing information in the blanks.

A I need to collect the customer satisfaction information now.

B Okay. Where did you get the ____________? From the latest ____________?

A Yes. I am looking at the results now.

B What is the main ____________ you see in the numbers?

A Customer happiness is going down this month.

B Oh no! Can you ____________ this month with the ____________ quarter?

A Yes, I will put them side-by-side in a chart.

B A chart is better than a table. Will you use a line ____________?

A Yes. And I will use a percentage to show how much the sales dropped.

B Great. When you ____________ the reason, please tell me immediately.

A I will. It looks like the problem is the price.

B We need to fix that fast!

6.7 Goal Questions

Find a position that you would like to apply to. Answer the questions to help you choose. Use the checklist to make sure you have all the information you need to proceed.

1 How can you collect and organize data?

2 What are the key results you need to interpret?

3 Which visual aids should you use to present data clearly?

4 What is one common mistake to avoid when discussing your findings?

5 Did the results confirm or falsify your initial hypotheses?

6.8 Task Checklist

Your assignment is to collect and organize customer data from your group survey. Interpret numerical results, trends, and percentages within the data. Use visual aids such as charts and graphs to present data clearly so you can create your report. It is important to organize your group members' tasks. Do not waste time.

☐	Collect Data	Collect the customer opinions in an organized way.
☐	Analyze Results	Check survey results to see if hypotheses were true or false.
☐	Identify Trend	Identify clear trends in the data.
☐	Compare Data Sets	Compare the data with customer groups.
☐	Use Visual Aids	Use charts or graphs as visual aids to explain the data easily.
☐	Use Percentages	Use percentages to describe the results.
☐	Find Interesting Results	Find any surprising or interesting results.
☐	Avoid Correlation/Causation	Ensure that correlation does not equal causation.
☐	Organize Variables	Organize the data into variables and control questions.
☐	Document Errors	Documented why hypotheses were false. Do not delete.

6.9 Good and Bad Data

Look at the two examples of data. How would you analyze them? Consider the questions with your partner. This Smart Watch Company is trying to make a new design. Why is this data insufficient? Why is the Data in Example B more likely to help our company sell more watches?

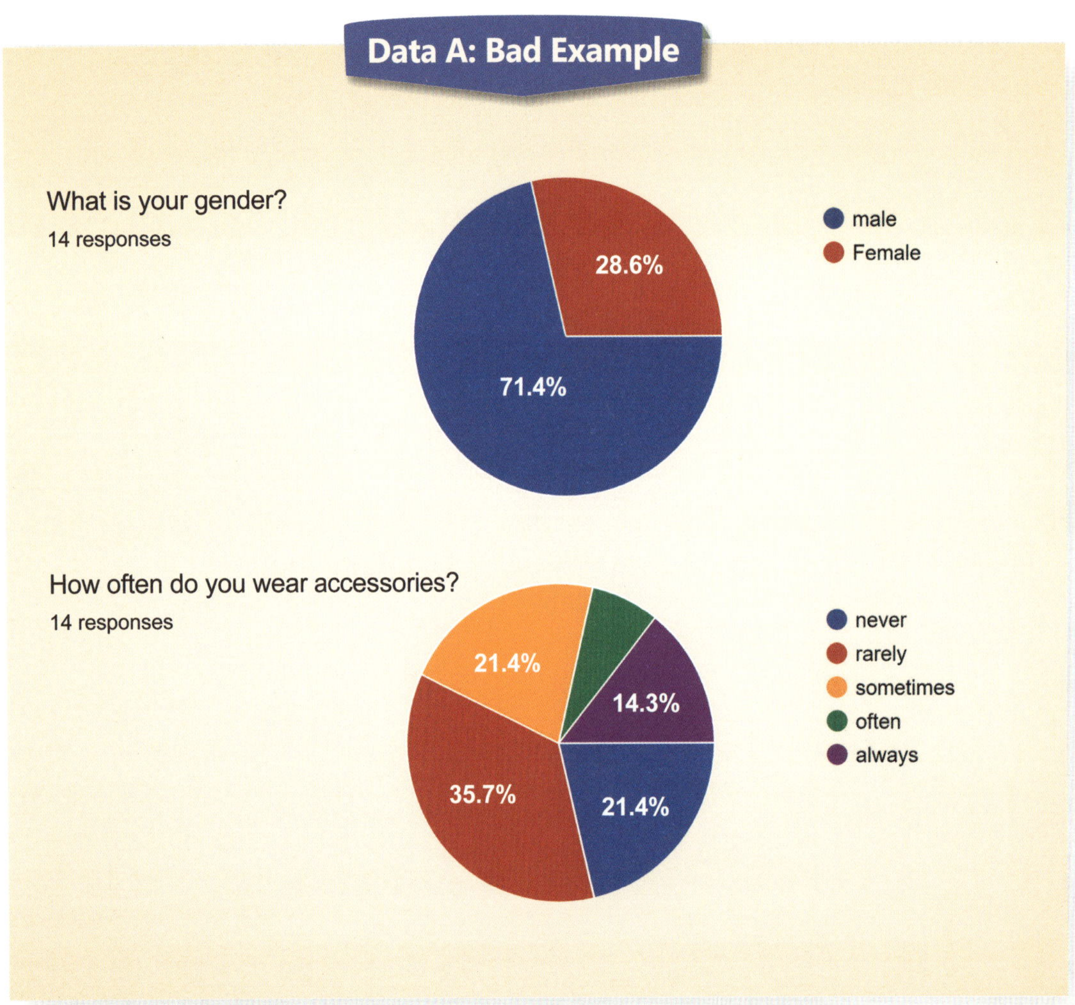

Discussion Questions

1 What is the problem with connecting the first graph with the second to test a hypothesis?

2 Does this data show that our accessory company should sell more smart watches to men?

3 What do we know from this data? How can we use it as evidence for a business strategy?

4 What do we learn from graph 2 about who might want to buy a new smart watch?

5 If we wanted to make two new watches for men and women, what other data do we need?

Data B: Good Example

What is your gender?	How often do you wear accessories?	What features of your smart device do you prefer?
Male	always	music
Female	always	music
Male	always	contact
Male	always	alarm
Male	always	music
Female	rarely	fitness function
Female	rarely	alarm
Female	rarely	music
Female	rarely	music
Male	rarely	contact
Female	rarely	fitness function
Female	never	contact

Discussion Questions

1 Why is this data easier to use?

2 How does the data in the middle column help us find customers?

3 If we want to make a new advertising campaign, how could we use the data in Column 3?

4 Use a pen to find trends in this data. What patterns can you find? (Find 3 patterns)

5 How could you organize the patterns in this data for your report and your presentation?

6.10 Unit Task

Collect and organize customer data from your group survey. Interpret numerical results, trends, and percentages within the data. Use visual aids such as charts and graphs to present data clearly, so you can create your report.

UNIT 7 Writing a Report

Reports are formal documents that present findings from your data analysis. You must write about the problem and suggest recommendations for action. A good report has a clear structure (including a title and a summary) and uses simple language so it is easy to read.

UNIT 7 Goals

- Learn the formal report structure.
- Write clearly and include necessary details.
- Present key findings and results.
- Offer recommendations for the company.

7.1 Discussion Questions

Discuss these questions with a partner. Write short keywords to help you remember your answers. Consider each question one at a time, answering each with your partner as you take notes.

1 What is the main goal of a business report? ______________________.

2 What is the conclusion in a report? ______________________.

3 What images can you use in a report? ______________________.

4 Why are headings important in a report? ______________________.

5 Should a report use long or simple words? ______________________.

7.2 Why is structure important in a report?

Clarity through Structure

A formal business report needs a strong structure to be easy to read. This document must use clear language. Every report needs a title (like "Office Security") and must clearly state the main topic. The short summary at the beginning helps the manager quickly read the main ideas before looking at every detail. Reports are often broken into numbered sections with clear headers.

Focusing on the Problem and Recommendations

The report is about the problem (like an old machine or high repair costs). You must include every necessary detail about the problem, such as the costs or history. The final conclusion section must summarize the main analysis. In the conclusion section, you must recommend the best course of action (for example, "I recommend buying a new one.") A good report needs to solve a problem and suggest improvements.

7.3 Fill-in-the-Blank Sentence

Use the words in the box to fill in the blanks.

conclusion	recommend	title	summary	problem
clear	section	page	topic	detail

1 The ______________ of my report is "Office Security."

2 The main ______________ of the report is the new computer system.

3 The report has three main ______________ .

4 In the ______________ , I will summarize the main ideas.

5 Please include every ______________ about the problem.

6 Read the short ______________ at the beginning to understand the report.

7 I wrote a five- ______________ report about the event.

8 I______________ that the company buys new chairs.

9 Please write in a way that is______________ and easy to read.

10 The report is about the______________ with the old machine.

7.4 Sentences with Vocabulary

Use the words on the left in a new sentence. This will help you use the word again later.

1	structure	Structure your report logically so it is easy to understand.
2	visualize	
3	convincing	
4	strategy	
5	correlation	

7.5 Report Standards

Read about reports and then answer the questions to check for understanding.

A. Structure and Clarity

Reports are formal documents that present the definitive findings from your data analysis. The report needs a strong structure to be easy to read and navigate. Since the findings are based on facts and numbers collected from surveys, the document must use clear language and simple words, as opposed to technical or complex vocabulary.

Every report needs a title (e.g., "Office Security Audit: Findings and Recommendations"). Crucially, it must include a short summary at the beginning for the manager to quickly read the main ideas before looking at every detail.

The body of the document should be broken into numbered sections with clear headers. This structure is necessary to guide the manager through the analytical process and the presented findings, ensuring they understand the interpretation of the numerical results.

Considerations for Structure and Clarity

- Write a clear and descriptive title.
- Include a short summary at the beginning for the manager to read quickly.
- Use a formal structure with clear headers for each section.
- Use clear and easy-to-read language.
- Check that the document is not too long or repetitive.

Comprehension Questions

1 Why is a strong structure necessary? ______________________.

2 What is the main purpose of the introduction? ______________________.

3 Why is easy-to-read language so important? ______________________.

4 How do numbered sections help a manager? ______________________.

5 How long should the report be? ______________________.

B. Problem Solving and Recommendations

The central purpose of the report is to solve a problem. The body of the report must clearly focus on the main problem and include necessary details about that problem, referencing the analyzed data and identified trends. It may be helpful to add a simple graph to help visualize your point.

The key findings from the data analysis should explain how you plan to solve the problem and suggest concrete improvements. Most importantly, in the conclusion section, you must recommend the best course of action.

A good report should show the manager where the company could develop and grow. The logical structuring of the data should make it easy to suggest improvements based on the facts and numbers analyzed. Consider the data as evidence and use it to prove your point.

Efficient group collaboration is also vital for success in dividing the complex writing tasks involved in producing a formal document. Make sure to give each person in your group a portion of the work. Begin the process by getting organized. Make a plan, and then you can work individually, collaborating independently on a shared document.

Considerations for Problem-solving and Recommendations

- Describe the main problem and include necessary details.
- Present the key findings (results from data analysis) clearly.
- Write a strong final conclusion that summarizes the analysis.
- Recommend the best course of action based on the findings.
- Suggest concrete improvements.

Comprehension Questions

1 How should you present the data? ____________________.

2 What must you include in the report body? ____________________.

3 How does efficient group collaboration help? ____________________.

4 What should you write in the conclusion? ____________________.

5 Why is it essential to support findings with data? ____________________.

7.6 Gap Fill A

With a partner choose one person to use Gap Fill A. Your partner will use Gap Fill B (in the back of the book). Practice the conversation with a partner and write the missing information in the blanks.

A I'm writing the final draft of the report about the old machine.

B What's a good ______________ for the document?

A I called it "Machine Efficiency and Repair Problems."

B Nice. Is the language very ______________ and easy to read?

A Yes, I used simple words. I included every detail about the costs.

B Good. I need to read the short ______________ first.

A That's ready. The first main section is about the machine's history.

B Okay. In the final ______________ , what do you ______________ ?

A I recommend buying a new one.

B That's a big decision! How many ______________ is the document?

A It's 10 pages long.

B And what is the main ______________ of the second section?

A It's about the repair costs.

B Okay, I will read it now.

7.7 Goal Questions

Write a formal report that is easy to read and tells the manager exactly what action they should take next. The report should highlight clear data that presents a plan to improve the company. Answer the questions and use the checklist to finish your report.

1 What structure should we use in our formal report?

2 What short summary should we write first for the manager to read quickly?

3 What action should we recommend in the Conclusion?

4 What details must be included about the problem our data and plan address?

5 How should we divide the work to be efficient?

7.8 Task Checklist

Your assignment is to write a clear formal business report. Include necessary details about how you plan to solve a problem and improve the company. Present key findings and offer recommendations for action to the reader. Practice efficient group collaboration by dividing tasks for report writing.

☐	Write Clear Title	Write a clear and descriptive title for the document.
☐	Include Summary	Write a short summary for the manager to read quickly.
☐	Describe Problem and Detail	Describe the main problem and include necessary details.
☐	Use Clear Structure	Use a formal structure with clear headers for each section.
☐	Present Key Findings	Present the key results from the data analysis.
☐	Write Strong Conclusion	Write a strong final conclusion that summarizes the analysis.
☐	Offer Recommendations	Recommend the best course of action in the conclusion.
☐	Use Simple Language	Use clear and easy-to-read language.
☐	Check Document Length	Check that the document is not too long.
☐	Collaborate Effectively	Practice efficient group collaboration by dividing writing tasks.

7.9 Good and Bad Report Findings

Look at the two report findings. These are examples of one part of the report. Read through the report and look at how the information is presented. Share your reactions with your group using the discussion questions.

Report A: Good Example

Finding 1: Daily Usage Indicates Strong Core Market and Opportunity
The majority of consumers view perfume as an everyday item, not just a luxury for special occasions. There is also an opportunity to grow sales by targeting professionals.

- **Strong Everyday Use**: Half of all respondents use perfume Anytime, confirming a strong core market for daily-use products. This suggests regular demand.
- **Romantic Scents**: The high percentage for On a date (40%) shows fragrance is strongly valued for social and emotional impact. Marketing campaigns should use this connection to sell to people for special moments like going on a date.
- **Growth Market for Professionals**: Only 10% use perfume during Working hours. This is a clear opportunity for the business to grow. We should develop and market light, professional scents to sell more perfume. We should design a campaign focused on working professionals.

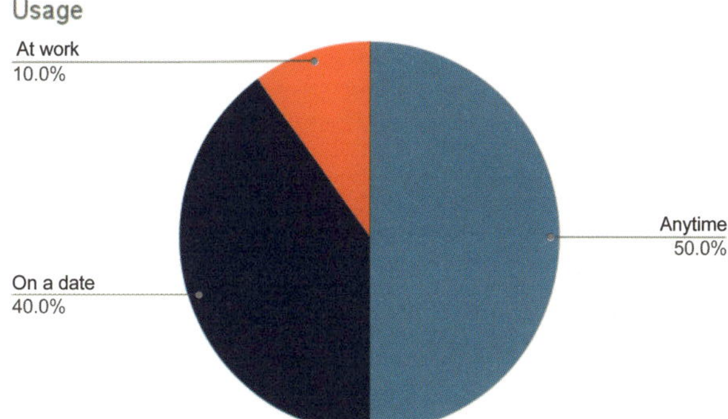

Conclusion: The data supports maintaining the popular daily-use market while launching a new line of subtle, work-appropriate scents to drive significant business growth.

Discussion Questions

1. How long did it take for you to read through this? Was this finding too long or too short?
2. Can you explain the plan in 3 steps? Do you think the manager will agree with the plan?
3. Do you think the report should include more numbers? What would you add?
4. Did you like the conclusion? Do you think there should have been anything else added?
5. Can you summarize the data by looking at the graph?

Report B: Bad Example

Finding 2: How People Say Bad Smells Are,

This part tell about smells that people no like. We must no use this smell for new perfume. The most bad smell is Pine and Strawberry (Sweet/Artificial). Many people say no to this smell. It get 160 answers, this is 43.8%. So we must stop use very sweet or fake fruit smell now.

Second bad smell is Spicy and Musk (Heavy). 120 people (32.9%) say no to this smell. This smell is too much strong and heavy. We must put less of this smell in perfume, is too much strong for many people.

Lavender smell is okay, 50 people (13.7%) no like it. But Citrus smell is the best smell, only 25 people (6.8%) no like. This citrus sniff is very safe to use.

Big idea: Many saram don't like sweet fake smells or strong heavy smells. We must make perfume that is fresh and clean for people to buy.

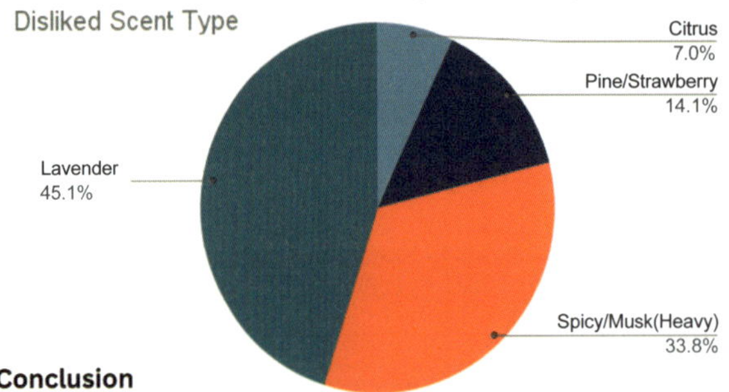

Conclusion

Look at survey answers. Market is changing fast for young people. They like perfume for good quality. Also the brand name and money is important for people. Man and woman like different smell. Woman like the fresh flower smell. Man people like soft smell. All people are different. Future time, we must make new things and better quality perfume. We must make our brand very big and strong. Must put advertisement on television and internet so many people can see. This is what we must do now fast. Finish.

Discussion Questions

1 How long did it take you to read this?

2 When did you look at the graph?

3 Does the hypothesis help you discuss your plan to improve the company?

4 What do you think the manager will take away from this written report finding?

5 How could you make the conclusion clearer?

7.10 Unit Task

Write a clear, formal business report. Include necessary details about how you plan to solve a problem and improve the company. Present key findings and offer recommendations for action to the reader. Practice efficient group collaboration by dividing tasks for report writing.

UNIT 8 Presenting Your Findings

The final step is presenting your report! You will practice speaking clearly and confidently to your audience. We will learn how to design effective slides using visual aids and keywords (not reading from a script) and how to use good body language and eye contact to deliver your information successfully.

UNIT 8 Goals

- Practice speaking to an audience confidently.
- Make effective presentation slides with visual aids.
- Use keywords instead of full scripts.
- Maintain good eye contact and body language.

8.1 Discussion Questions

Discuss these questions with a partner. Write short keywords to help you remember your answers. Consider each question one at a time, answering each with your partner as you take notes.

1 Do you feel nervous when you present? ____________________.

2 Should you read every word from slides? ____________________.

3 What should you do with your hands? ____________________.

4 What should you say when you finish? ____________________.

5 How can you engage the audience? ____________________.

8.2 How should you prepare your slides and speak?

Keywords and Visual Aids

A presentation should not be a scripted, monotone lecture. The worst thing you can do is read every word from a script. You should use visual aids, like pictures, charts, and graphs, on your slides. Use keywords instead of full sentences to help you remember what to speak about. You should also try to use more slides with less information on each one. These methods help you explain the data clearly.

Confidence and Connecting with the Audience

When presenting your report findings, you must speak clearly and confidently. The audience needs to trust you. Strong eye contact with the people in the room is important to engage them. You should introduce yourself and the findings at the beginning. It is a good practice to prepare handouts (paper copies) of the main points for the audience. At the end, you should always finish strong. Do not make a long, boring summary. Review your main points in short, simple sentences. Thank the audience to finish the presentation.

8.3 Fill-in-the-Blank Sentence

Use the words in the box to fill in the blanks.

introduce	confidently	slide	speak	audience
visual	explain	eye contact	question	handout

1 The______________ listened quietly to my talk.

2 I need to______________ loudly so everyone can hear me.

3 I put a photo on the first______________ of my presentation.

4 Can you______________ the difficult words on the chart?

5 The pictures and charts are called______________ aids.

6 I need to______________ myself before I start talking.

7 Good______________ means looking at the people in the room.

8 I gave the______________ (paper copy) to everyone before the talk.

9 Please feel free to ask a______________ after I finish.

10 You must______________ (with confidence) tell people your results.

8.4 Sentences with Vocabulary

Use the words on the left in a new sentence. This will help you use the word again later.

1	reliable	Make sure your information is presented with confidence to make it more reliable.
2	engage	
3	organize	
4	display	
5	utilize	

8.5 Presentation Standards

Read about what and how you should present your project and then answer the questions below to check for understanding.

A. Slides and Speaking Style

When giving a presentation, you must speak clearly and confidently to engage the audience. The presentation must not be a scripted, monotone lecture, and you should avoid reading every word from a script, as this is viewed as unprofessional and hinders connection with the audience.

Instead, your slides should primarily use keywords to help you remember what to speak about and guide your audience. You must use strong visual aids, like pictures, charts, and graphs, which clearly present the numerical data and identified trends. These aids help you explain complex findings without having to rely on long paragraphs of text.

A strong rule for slide design is efficiency: you should use more slides with less information on each one. This prevents the audience from being overwhelmed by text and forces you, the presenter, to focus on the key takeaways and speak to the facts and numbers you analyzed.

Considerations for Slides and Speaking

- Practice speaking clearly and confidently without relying on a script.
- Avoid reading every word from a script.
- Use keywords on slides (not full sentences).
- Use strong visual aids (charts and graphs) to explain data.
- Use more slides with less information on each one.

Comprehension Questions

1 Why is reading every word from a script bad? ______________________.

2 How do keywords on your slides help you? ______________________.

3 What is the purpose of using more slides? ______________________.

4 How do visual aids help you present? ______________________.

5 Should you practice your presentation? ______________________.

B. Audience Engagement and Confidence

To succeed, you must ensure the audience trusts you. Strong eye contact with the people in the room is important to engage them directly. Good presentation etiquette also involves using appropriate body language (e.g., standing tall, using controlled gestures).

Your structure should be welcoming: You should introduce yourself and preview the report findings at the beginning. It is also good practice to prepare handouts (paper copies) of the main points for the audience, providing them with a physical reference to follow along.

At the end, you must finish strong. Review your main points in short, simple sentences, and thank the audience. This step is crucial because it ensures the audience remembers the main conclusion and prevents the presentation from ending with a long, confusing summary. Your confident presentation style reinforces the credibility of the report's findings.

One way you can become more confident in a group presentation is to plan your turns. When presenting with a group, no one should be waiting or doing nothing. Keep each person actively engaged or you will risk boring the audience. Use your group to share the mic. Take many short turns rather than having long speaking turns for each person. Keep your presentation moving quickly or your audience will fall asleep.

Considerations for Engagement and Confidence

- Make strong eye contact with the audience to engage them.
- Introduce yourself and preview report findings early.
- Use appropriate body language and gestures.
- Prepare by organizing your group's turn-taking.
- Finish strong with a short summary and thank the audience.

Comprehension Questions

1 Why is strong eye contact essential? ______________________.

2 Why are short, simple sentences helpful? ______________________.

3 What does it mean to finish strong? ______________________.

4 How should you start the presentation? ______________________.

5 How does body language show confidence? ______________________.

8.6 Gap Fill A

With a partner choose one person to use Gap Fill A. Your partner will use Gap Fill B (in the back of the book). Practice the conversation with a partner and write the missing information in the blanks.

A I am ready to introduce my report findings to the team.

B Great. I hope the ______________ is interested!

A I hope so, too. I will speak clearly and confidently.

B That's the most important thing.

A I have 10 main points, so I made 10 slides.

B Good. I like that you used many ______________ aids, like pictures.

A Yes, they help to explain the data better than just words.

B They do. Remember to make strong ___________ ___________ with the room.

A I will. I also made handouts for everyone to take home.

B Excellent idea. At the end, don't forget to take ______________ .

A Right. I'll save 5 minutes for that.

B I think you are totally prepared.

8.7 Goal Questions

Prepare your presentation. Use keywords and visual aids, not a script, to introduce and explain your findings to the audience. Answer the questions to help you prepare. Use the checklist to make sure you have all the information you need to present.

1. How can we make slides simple and engaging?
2. How can we engage the audience?
3. How can we make it easy to remember what we want to say?
4. What key visuals should be included in our presentation to make it easy to understand?
5. How should we take turns speaking?

8.8 Task Checklist

Your assignment is to introduce and explain report findings clearly and confidently to an audience. Design effective presentation slides using keywords and visual aids, not full scripts. Practice presentation etiquette including appropriate body language and eye contact with your audience. Remember to spend more time practicing your speaking than preparing a complex PPT file. In your test, you will be speaking to your coworkers and boss. Practice speaking confidently and organize your presentation to look professional in public.

☐	Practice Speaking Confidently	Practice speaking clearly and confidently to the audience.
☐	Use Keywords (No Script)	Design slides using keywords and avoid reading from a script.
☐	Use Visual Aids	Use visual aids (charts and graphs) to explain the report data.
☐	Maintain Eye Contact	Make strong eye contact with the audience.
☐	Introduce Topic	Introduce yourself professionally and preview report findings.
☐	Manage Speaking Time	Manage speaking time efficiently.
☐	Prepare PPT	Prepare a minimal PPT to highlight main points.
☐	Finish Strong	Finish with a short sentence and thank the audience.
☐	Practice Turn-taking	Practice taking turns speaking with your group members.
☐	Prioritize Practice	Spend more time practicing speaking than preparing a PPT file.

8.9 Good and Bad Slides

Look at the slides below. Consider what is good and bad about both. Use the discussion questions to help you analyze them with a partner. Refer to the back of the book for possible answers to the questions.

Slide A: Bad Example

DATA ANALYSIS

TRUE

HYPOTHESIS 1

Our overarching HYPOTHESIS for this quarterly effort was that: The perceived temporal disconnect between intra-departmental resource request submission and the tangible fulfillment of those requests, as moderated by exogenous variables related to desk ergonomic quality, will exhibit an inverse, non-linear correlation with reported long-term employee retention likelihood, provided that ambient office lighting remains within the 450 to 550 lumen range.

HYPOTHESIS 3

We found that our hypothesis was true because we asked 100 people and 54 said yes. Question 1 was how old are you. Everyone answered that they are 22. Question 2 was good too because we asked: "Do you like our product?" 10 people answered no, 3 people answered maybe and 87 people answered yes. So Hypothesis 3 was true.

HYPOTHESIS 2

Question: "Do you feel that the company has recently (within the last 90 days) made a noticeable investment in employee comfort and ergonomic well-being?" A promising 40% of the respondents have positively affirmed our perception of investment. This is good news, even though we haven't actually made any new investments in the last 90 days. Their perception is the reality we are trying to create. The majority (60%) feel we have made no noticeable investment. This strongly validates the 40% who said 'Yes,' as it proves that perceptions are subjective and highly variable across the organizational matrix. This finding reinforces the need for more subjective surveys.

Discussion Questions

1 What words would you keep from this slide? What would you delete or add?

2 Do you think the manager cares about your hypotheses in your report? Why or why not?

3 How many slides should this information really need?

4 Why is long, overly complex analysis a bad way to present your data?

5 How does the slide design make you feel about the group's work?

Slide B: Good Example

This group is presenting their new line of cosmetics. They are exploring the growing market of male customers. The survey was given to students at a local university. Look at how they designed their slide and discuss the questions below with your group.

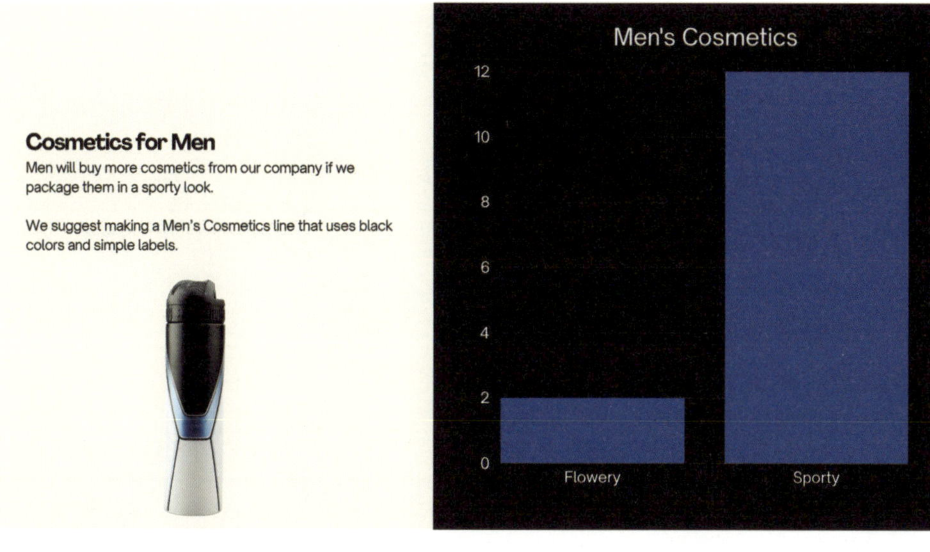

Discussion Questions

1 What do you notice first about this slide?

2 If your group was using this slide, what would you say to the audience?

3 Do you think the image is easy to understand?

4 What do you think the manager will remember about this slide/presentation?

5 Could you improve this slide in any way? If so, how?

8.10 Unit Task

Introduce and explain your findings clearly and confidently to an audience. Design effective presentation slides using keywords and visual aids, not full scripts. Practice presentation etiquette including appropriate body language and eye contact with your audience. Remember to spend more time practicing your speaking than preparing a complex PPT file. In your test, you will be speaking to your coworkers and boss. Practice speaking confidently and organize your presentation to look professional in public.

Appendix

Vocabulary Practice

Unit 1 Vocabulary

Word	Korean	Sentence
opening		
salary		
unemployed		
colleague		
advertisement		
apply		
workplace		
qualifications		
part-time		
skills		
preferences		
valuable		
competitive		
experience		
degree		

Unit 2 Vocabulary

Word	Korean	Sentence
résumé		
previous		
summary		
accomplishment		
experience		
contact		
skills		
objective		
format		
header		
education		
bullet points		
chronological		
trustworthy		
customized		

Unit 3 Vocabulary

Word	Korean	Sentence
formal		
greeting		
vacancy		
dear		
sincerely		
closing		
manager		
position		
enclosed		
enthusiastic		
etiquette		
polite		
impression		
formatting		
cover letter		

Unit 4 Vocabulary

Word	Korean	Sentence
interview		
answer		
strength		
weakness		
dress		
punctual		
practice		
gesture		
body language		
confidently		
professional		
keywords		
research		
firm		
question		

Unit 5 Vocabulary

Word	Korean	Sentence
proposal		
suggest		
hypotheses		
request		
goal		
introduction		
approval		
project		
budget		
solution		
benefits		
timeline		
convincing		
strategy		
explicit		

Unit 6 Vocabulary

Word	Korean	Sentence
data		
analysis		
causation		
collect		
graph		
trend		
compare		
chart		
result		
survey		
information		
numerical		
visual aids		
interpret		
percentage		

Unit 7 Vocabulary

Word	Korean	Sentence
report		
title		
collaborate		
state		
improve		
formal		
correlation		
findings		
problem		
section		
conclusion		
topic		
clear		
recommend		
detail		

Unit 8 Vocabulary

Word	Korean	Sentence
speak		
introduce		
explain		
visual		
slide		
effective		
handout		
nervous		
eye contact		
presentation		
review		
script		
engagement		
display		
audience		

Fill-in the Blank Answer Key

1.3 Blanks

1. salary
2. boss
3. workplace
4. apply
5. opening
6. part-time
7. colleague
8. experience
9. advertisement
10. Unemployed

2.3 Blanks

1. summary
2. objective
3. previous
4. date
5. accomplishment
6. University
7. contact
8. format
9. skills
10. photo

3.3 Blanks

1. dear
2. enclosed
3. sincerely
4. formal
5. position
6. greeting
7. opening
8. enthusiastic
9. closing
10. manager

4.3 Blanks

1. question
2. answer
3. weakness
4. strength
5. punctual
6. research
7. dress
8. body language
9. firm
10. practice

5.3 Blanks

1. suggest
2. budget
3. solution
4. project
5. benefits
6. request
7. approval
8. timeline
9. introduction
10. goal

6.3 Blanks

1. information
2. result
3. chart
4. trend
5. percentage
6. survey
7. compare
8. find
9. collect
10. graph

7.3 Blanks

1. title
2. topic
3. section
4. conclusion
5. detail
6. summary
7. page
8. recommend
9. clear
10. problem

8.3 Blanks

1. audience
2. speak
3. slide
4. explain
5. visual
6. introduce
7. eye contact
8. handout
9. question
10. confidently

Gap Fill B

1. Find a Job

Gap Fill B

Practice the conversation with a partner and write the missing information in the blanks.

A I saw a new job __________ yesterday. I think I will __________ for it.

B Oh, nice! Is it a full-time opening?

A Yes. It's a good step up. I've been __________ for too long.

B I know that feeling! Did they say what the salary is?

A They listed a good range. It's better than my __________ job.

B That's good news. What kind of experience are they looking for?

A They want experience in customer service, which I have a lot of.

B Perfect. I hope the new boss is nice, though.

A Me too. My last one was terrible!

B And you need a friendly colleague to work with, right?

A Absolutely! I just want a better __________ than before.

B I understand. Are you applying for a full-time or a part-time job?

A Full-time. I need the hours.

B Well, I hope you get an interview soon!

A Thanks! I'm sending the application now.

B Good luck!

2. Write a Résumé

Gap Fill B

Practice the conversation with a partner and write the missing information in the blanks.

A My résumé needs work. Is this ____________ okay?

B It looks neat. Let's check your education section first.

A I put the university graduation ____________ there.

B Perfect. Now for the work history section.

A Yes. I listed all my ____________ job titles here.

B Good. And did you list your biggest accomplishment at your last job?

A Yes, I ____________ that I saved the company money.

B Excellent. You must include a short summary at the very top.

A I did! Below that, I wrote my career ____________ .

B Great. You clearly need to list your language skill.

A I said I ____________ English and Spanish.

B Fantastic. What about the people for your references?

A I have three people. Do I put their ____________ details on the page?

B No, just say "References available upon request."

A Okay, that's better.

B It looks ready to send!

3. Write a Cover Letter

Gap Fill B

Practice the conversation with a partner and write the missing information in the blanks.

A I'm writing the cover letter now. I'll start with the proper ___________ .

B Good. Remember to write "Dear Mr. Smith," not "Hello."

A Right. I must keep the whole style very ___________ .

B Exactly. The tone is important for a business letter.

A My ___________ explains why I am ___________ about the job.

B That's great! Enthusiasm helps.

A I clearly wrote the job ___________ I want in the first line.

B Smart. Did you mention that your résumé is enclosed?

A Yes, I did. I hope the hiring ___________ reads it soon.

B Me too. What are you writing for the final closing?

A I plan to use the word " ___________ ."

B That is the correct formal word to use.

A I also added a sentence about waiting for their call.

B Perfect. It sounds professional.

A Thanks for checking!

B No problem.

4. Prepare for a Job Interview

Gap Fill B

Practice the conversation with a partner and write the missing information in the blanks.

A I'm so scared about the job ____________ today.

B Don't be! You just need to be punctual. Arrive 10 minutes early.

A I will. I also need to remember to ____________ smartly.

B Yes, professional clothes are a must.

A I spent an hour yesterday trying to ________ their common ________ .

B Good. Did you research the company's latest news?

A Yes, I read everything on their website.

B Perfect. What did you decide to say is your biggest strength?

A I'll say I'm great at solving ____________ .

B Excellent. And how will you explain your weakness?

A I'll say I work too hard, but I am learning to rest.

B That's a good answer. Remember to practice a firm handshake.

A I will. And I'll smile to show good ________ ________ .

B You've got this!

5. Proposals

Gap Fill B

Practice the conversation with a partner and write the missing information in the blanks.

A I finished the plan. I will ____________ it to the board tomorrow.

B Great. You mean the new software proposal?

A Yes. The main ________ is to find a ________ to our slow system.

B That's important. How big is the project?

A It's a 3-month project. We need a large ________ for new equipment.

B Okay. I hope you get their approval quickly.

A I need to show them the amazing ________ of the software.

B That's right. What about the timeline?

A I included one that shows every step by week.

B Excellent. Did you clearly state the request for the money?

A Yes, it's at the end.

B And is there a good introduction?

A Yes, it clearly states the software ____________ .

B Perfect. They will love it.

6. Analyzing Data

Gap Fill B

Practice the conversation with a partner and write the missing information in the blanks.

A I need to __________ the customer satisfaction __________ now.

B Okay. Where did you get the data? From the latest survey?

A Yes. I am looking at the ____________ now.

B What is the main trend you see in the numbers?

A Customer happiness is going down this month.

B Oh no! Can you compare this month with the previous quarter?

A Yes, I will put them side-by-side in a ____________.

B A chart is better than a table. Will you use a line graph?

A Yes. And I will use a __________ to show how much the sales dropped.

B Great. When you find the reason, please tell me immediately.

A I will. It looks like the problem is the price.

B We need to fix that fast!

7. Writing a Report

Gap Fill B

Practice the conversation with a partner and write the missing information in the blanks.

A I'm writing the final draft of the__________ about the old machine.

B What's a good title for the document?

A I called it "Machine Efficiency and Repair__________ ."

B Nice. Is the language very clear and easy to read?

A Yes, I used simple words. I included every__________ about the costs.

B Good. I need to read the short summary first.

A That's ready. The first main__________ is about the machine's history.

B Okay. In the final conclusion, what do you recommend?

A I recommend buying a new one.

B That's a big decision! How many pages is the document?

A It's 10 pages long.

B And what is the main topic of the second section?

A It's about the repair costs.

B Okay, I will read it now.

8. Presenting Your Findings

Gap Fill B

Practice the conversation with a partner and write the missing information in the blanks.

A I am ready to____________ my report findings to the team.

B Great. I hope the audience is interested!

A I hope so too. I will __________ clearly and __________ .

B That's the most important thing.

A I have 10 main points, so I made 10 ____________ .

B Good. I like that you used many visual aids, like pictures.

A Yes, they help to ____________ the data better than just words.

B They do. Remember to make strong eye contact with the room.

A I will. I also made ____________ for everyone to take home.

B Excellent idea. At the end, don't forget to ask questions.

A Right. I'll save 5 minutes for that.

B I think you are totally prepared.

Test Rubrics

Job Interview Rubric

Categories	1 Point (Needs Work: Not Ready)	3 Points (Good: Okay)	5 Points (Excellent: Very Good)	Score
1 Preparation	Does not research the company or bring the needed documents.	Researches the company, but forgets to bring copies of documents.	Researches the company well and brings copies of the Résumé/Cover Letter.	
2 Answer Content	Answers are vague or focus on weakness/ unimportant things.	Answers are clear but sometimes miss keywords or details about experience.	Answers quickly and focuses on great strengths, using keywords from the résumé.	
3 Delivery	Reads answers from a script or speaks unclearly.	Speaks clearly but pauses too much or seems a little nervous.	Speaks clearly and confidently without reading from a script.	
4 Body Language	Looks awkward, avoids eye contact, or sits poorly.	Has good posture and smiles, but forgets the handshake or appropriate gestures.	Sits straight, smiles, uses correct gestures, and gives a firm handshake.	
5 Professionalism	Is late or wears clothes that are not professional.	Is exactly on time, but forgets to plan a thank you email.	Is punctual (arrives 10 minutes early) and plans to send a thank-you email.	

Presentation Rubric

Categories	1 Point (Needs Work: Not Ready)	3 Points (Good: Okay)	5 Points (Excellent: Very Good)	Score
1 Slide Design	Slides are full of long, dense text or have no visual aids.	Uses charts but has too much information or text on some slides.	Uses visual aids (charts/graphs) and uses more slides with less information.	
2 Speaking Style	Reads the full script or reads every word on the slides.	Sometimes reads from the slide text but mostly uses keywords.	Speaks using keywords and does not read every word from a script.	
3 Delivery	Speaks in a low, monotone voice and seems nervous.	Speaks clearly but sometimes speaks too quietly or quickly.	Speaks clearly and confidently (loudly) to engage the audience.	
4 Audience Connection	Avoids looking at the audience (looks at the floor or the wall).	Makes some eye contact but looks at the slides or notes too much.	Makes strong eye contact with the audience and uses appropriate body language.	
5 Structure	Does not introduce the topic or forgets to thank the audience at the end.	Has a clear start and finish, but the final summary is too long.	Introduces the findings clearly, manages time, and finishes strong with a short thank-you.	

Gap Fill Answers

1 Find a Job

A I saw a new job **advert** yesterday. I think I will **apply** for it.

B Oh, nice! Is it a full-time **opening**?

A Yes. It's a good step up. I've been **unemployed** for too long.

B I know that feeling! Did they say what the **salary** is?

A They listed a good range. It's better than my **previous** job.

B That's good news. What kind of **experience** are they looking for?

A They want experience in customer service, which I have a lot of.

B Perfect. I hope the new **boss** is nice, though.

A Me too. My last one was terrible!

B And you need a friendly **colleague** to work with, right?

A Absolutely! I just want a better **workplace** than before.

B I understand. Are you applying for a full-time or a **part-time** job?

A Full-time. I need the hours.

B Well, I hope you get an interview soon!

A Thanks! I'm sending the application now.

B Good luck!

2. Write a Résumé

A My résumé needs work. Is this **format** okay?

B It looks neat. Let's check your **education** section first.

A I put the university graduation **date** there.

B Perfect. Now for the work **history** section.

A Yes. I listed all my **previous** job titles here.

B Good. And did you list your biggest **accomplishment** at your last job?

A Yes, I **added** that I saved the company money.

B Excellent. You must include a short **summary** at the very top.

A I did! Below that, I wrote my career **objective**.

B Great. You clearly need to list your language **skill**.

A I said I **speak** English and Spanish.

B Fantastic. What about the people for your **references**?

A I have three people. Do I put their **contact** details on the page?

B No, just say "**References available upon request**."

A Okay, that's better.

B It looks ready to send!

3. Write a Cover Letter

A I'm writing the cover letter now. I'll start with the proper **greeting**.

B Good. Remember to write "**Dear** Mr. Smith," not "Hello."

A Right. I must keep the whole style very **formal**.

B Exactly. The tone is important for a business letter.

A My **opening** explains why I am **enthusiastic** about the job.

B That's great! Enthusiasm helps.

A I clearly wrote the job **position** I want in the first line.

B Smart. Did you mention that your résumé is **enclosed**?

A Yes, I did. I hope the hiring **manager** reads it soon.

B Me too. What are you writing for the final **closing**?

A I plan to use the word "**Sincerely**."

B That is the correct formal word to use.

A I also added a sentence about waiting for their call.

B Perfect. It sounds professional.

A Thanks for checking!

B No problem.

4. Prepare for a Job Interview

A I'm so scared about the job **interview** today.

B Don't be! You just need to be **punctual**. Arrive 10 minutes early.

A I will. I also need to remember to **dress** smartly.

B Yes, professional clothes are a must.

A I spent an hour yesterday trying to **answer** their common **questions**.

B Good. Did you **research** the company's latest news?

A Yes, I read everything on their website.

B Perfect. What did you decide to say is your biggest **strength**?

A I'll say I'm great at solving **problems**.

B Excellent. And how will you explain your **weakness**?

A I'll say I work too hard, but I am learning to rest.

B That's a good answer. Remember to **practice** a **firm** handshake.

A I will. And I'll smile to show good **body language**.

B You've got this!

5. Proposals

A I finished the plan. I will **suggest** it to the board tomorrow.

B Great. You mean the new software **proposal**?

A Yes. The main **goal** is to find a **solution** to our slow system.

B That's important. How big is the **project**?

A It's a 3-month project. We need a large **budget** for new equipment.

B Okay. I hope you get their **approval** quickly.

A I need to show them the amazing **benefits** of the software.

B That's right. What about the **timeline**?

A I included one that shows every step by week.

B Excellent. Did you clearly state the **request** for the money?

A Yes, it's at the end.

B And is there a good **introduction**?

A Yes, it clearly states the software **problem**.

B Perfect. They will love it.

6. Analyzing Data

A I need to **collect** the customer satisfaction **information** now.

B Okay. Where did you get the **data**? From the latest **survey**?

A Yes. I am looking at the **results** now.

B What is the main **trend** you see in the numbers?

A Customer happiness is going down this month.

B Oh no! Can you **compare** this month with the **previous** quarter?

A Yes, I will put them side-by-side in a **chart**.

B A chart is better than a table. Will you use a line **graph**?

A Yes. And I will use a **percentage** to show how much the sales dropped.

B Great. When you **find** the reason, please tell me immediately.

A I will. It looks like the problem is the price.

B We need to fix that fast!

7. Writing a Report

A I'm writing the final draft of the **report** about the old machine.

B What's a good **title** for the document?

A I called it "Machine Efficiency and Repair **Problems**."

B Nice. Is the language very **clear** and easy to read?

A Yes, I used simple words. I included every **detail** about the costs.

B Good. I need to read the short **summary** first.

A That's ready. The first main **section** is about the machine's history.

B Okay. In the final **conclusion**, what do you **recommend**?

A I recommend buying a new one.

B That's a big decision! How many **pages** is the document?

A It's 10 pages long.

B And what is the main **topic** of the second section?

A It's about the repair costs.

B Okay, I will read it now.

8. Presenting Your Findings

A I am ready to **introduce** my report findings to the team.

B Great. I hope the **audience** is interested!

A I hope so, too. I will **speak** clearly and **confidently**.

B That's the most important thing.

A I have 10 main points, so I made 10 **slides**.

B Good. I like that you used many **visual** aids, like pictures.

A Yes, they help to **explain** the data better than just words.

B They do. Remember to make strong **eye contact** with the room.

A I will. I also made **handouts** for everyone to take home.

B Excellent idea. At the end, don't forget to take **questions**.

A Right. I'll save 5 minutes for that.

B I think you are totally prepared.

Notes

Notes

Notes

Notes

Notes

Notes

Notes

Notes

WORK **SMARTER** 3rd Edition

2026. 2. 4. 3판 1쇄 인쇄
2026. 2. 11. 3판 1쇄 발행

지은이 | Lowell Sanborn
펴낸이 | 이종춘
펴낸곳 | BM (주)도서출판 성안당
주소 | 04032 서울시 마포구 양화로 127 첨단빌딩 3층(출판기획 R&D 센터)
10881 경기도 파주시 문발로 112 파주 출판 문화도시(제작 및 물류)
전화 | 02) 3142-0036
031) 950-6300
팩스 | 031) 955-0510
등록 | 1973. 2. 1. 제406-2005-000046호
출판사 홈페이지 | www.cyber.co.kr
ISBN | 978-89-315-8475-2 (13740)
정가 | 20,000원

이 책을 만든 사람들
책임 | 최옥현
진행 | 공정환, 김은주
기획 · 편집 | 김은주
교정 · 교열 | 김은주, 박가현
본문 · 표지 디자인 | 임흥순
홍보 | 김계향, 임진성, 김주승, 최정민
국제부 | 이선민, 조혜란
마케팅 | 구본철, 차정욱, 오영일, 나진호, 강호묵
마케팅 지원 | 장상범
제작 | 김유석

■ **도서 A/S 안내**

성안당에서 발행하는 모든 도서는 저자와 출판사, 그리고 독자가 함께 만들어 나갑니다.
좋은 책을 펴내기 위해 많은 노력을 기울이고 있습니다. 혹시라도 내용상의 오류나 오탈자 등이 발견되면 **"좋은 책은 나라의 보배"**로서 우리 모두가 함께 만들어 간다는 마음으로 연락주시기 바랍니다. 수정 보완하여 더 나은 책이 되도록 최선을 다하겠습니다.
성안당은 늘 독자 여러분들의 소중한 의견을 기다리고 있습니다. 좋은 의견을 보내주시는 분께는 성안당 쇼핑몰의 포인트(3,000포인트)를 적립해 드립니다.

잘못 만들어진 책이나 부록 등이 파손된 경우에는 교환해 드립니다.